QUETZALCOATL
THE BEARDED WHITE GOD OF ANCIENT AMERICA

THE BEARDED WHITE GOD
OF ANCIENT AMERICA

QUETZALCOATL

COMPILED BY

DONALD W. HEMINGWAY

W. DAVID HEMINGWAY

ISBN: 1-55517-777-8
e. 1

Published by CFI
an imprint of Cedar Fort Inc.
www.cedarfort.com

Distributed by:

Cover design by Nicole Shaffer
Cover design © 2004 by Lyle Mortimer

Printed in the United States of America
10 9 8 7 6 5 4 3 2 1

Printed on acid-free paper

To all those who seek to learn of Jesus Christ.

We are grateful to the libraries and kind staff of the University of Utah and The Church of Jesus Christ of Latter-day Saints for their help in our research for this book.

Contents

Foreword

Hernando Cortes' Conquest of the Aztecs 1

Fernando de Alva Ixtlilxochitl 37

Don Mariano Fernandez de Echeverria y Veytia 50
    Cataclysm at the Death of Jesus Christ 50
    The Coming of Quetzalcohuatl 54
    Quetzalcoatl Thought to Have Been an Apostle 61
    Doctrines and Rites Quetzalcoatl Taught 68
    Two Famous Prophecies Made by Quetzalcohuatl 83

Hubert Howe Bancroft 90
    Quetzalcoatl Identified as Christ 91
    Arguments Identfying Quetxocoatl with the Messiah 92
    Theories on Origin of Native Americans 93

William Hickling Prescott 96

Lord Edward King Kingsborough 99

Who Was Qutezalcoatl? 113

Appendix I: LDS President John Taylor
    on Quetzalcoatl 123

Appendix II: Exerpts of the Book of Mormon
    that Account for the Quetzalcoatl Myth 124
    Advent of Jesus Christ 127
    Cataclysm 129
    Appearance and Teachings of Jesus Christ 136

References 177

Index 181

FOREWORD

After it [Book of Mormon] *had come forth unto them I beheld other books, which came forth by the power of the Lamb, from the Gentiles unto them, unto the convincing of the Gentiles and the remnant of the seed of my brethren, and also the Jews who were scattered upon all the face of the earth, that the records of the prophets and the twelve apostles of the Lamb are true* (Book of Mormon, 1 Nephi, 13:39).

In the ancient history of Mexico and other parts of early America as recorded by many writers—natives, Spanish conquistadores, Spanish priests, historians, and others—there appears the name and relation of the visitation of Quetzalcohautl, often referred to as The Bearded White God. Mariano Veytia, celebrated Mexican historian (1720-1778), wrote: "Among all the authors who have written of the Indies, there is none who does not talk about this wonderful man" (Ancient America Rediscovered, 152). Who was he, when did he appear, where did he come from, why did he come, what did he teach, where did he go?

From these writings about Quetzalcohuatl this book has been compiled.

NOTE

Names of persons and places are spelled differently by writers quoted in this book—for example, Quetzalcohuatl, Quetzalacoatl, Quecalcoatle and Montezuma, Moctezuma, Motecuhcuma. We have retained the original spelling of each writer.

Hernando Cortes' Conquest of the Aztecs

As reported by Cortes, his associates, and contemporaries

One of the greatest military victories in the history of the world was the conquest of the Aztec nation by Spanish Conquistadores. Hernando Cortes with a handful of soldiers subdued the mighty Mexican empire.

When one looks at the Aztec armed forces numbering in tens of thousands, militaristic judgment would have condemned the Spanish adventurers to foolhardy destruction before they began. "Never did a captain with such a small army do such deeds, win so many victories, and win so vast an empire" (Gomara, 23).

From another early writer, Fray Toribio Motolinia, a Spanish Franciscan friar, said to have arrived in Mexico in 1524, we read: "Although the Spaniards conquered this land by force of arms (in which conquest God showed many marvels—that so great a land should be won by so few when the natives had many weapons, both offensive and defensive); and although the Spaniards burned some temples of the devil and broke some idols, it was very little in comparison with what remained; God has therefore showed His power still more in having held this land with such small numbers as the Spaniards had. Many times when the natives had the opportunity to recover their land with great facility and ease, God blinded their understanding, and at other times when they have been bound and united for this purpose (i.e., the recovery of their land), and all in agreement, God miraculously upset their plans. If God permitted them to begin this undertaking, they would easily be able to carry it out, being all united and of the same mind and having many Spanish weapons" (Motolinia, 89).

WHO WAS CORTES?

Hernan Cortes was born in 1485 in Medellin, province of Extremadura, Spain. His parents were poor as to the goods of this world but rich in that they came from ancient, noble and honorable ancestral lines. They were loved and esteemed by their neighbors. For a time his father served in the army as a lieutenant in a company of horsemen.

As a child Cortes was very sickly, many times at the point of death, but through care and prayers he was strengthened and healed. While yet in his crib his nanny placed before him the names of the Twelve Apostles and Cortes selected St. Peter as his special advocate.

Doting parents proudly watched their son grow and planned for his bright future. He should have a fine career in the field of law. Following this plan, at the age of fourteen he was sent to Salamanca to live with an aunt and study at the university. But after two years he returned home weary of his studies, or possibly from lack of money, to the great disappointment of his parents.

At home, as a teen-ager, he was a source of never-ending trouble to his parents, being restless, haughty, mischievous and given to quarreling. Neither he nor they could decide what he should do. During this period he is said to have worked for a year in the office of a Notary gaining valuable experience. This kind of employment, however, was not satisfying to this restless youth as he desired to seek his fortune in the world. He soon set out for Italy, but hearing of Columbus' discovery he turned his eyes and desires toward the Indies (newly discovered America). At nineteen, in 1504, he took a voyage toward the new world landing in Santo Domingo, now known as the Dominican Republic. For a time he settled down being appointed Notary of a local town. He also carried on trading and merchandising.

Within several years his restless spirit sought further adventure, and he joined with Diego Velasquez in the conquest of Cuba. He was clerk of the treasurer in the expedition. After the conquest Velasquez gave him a settlement of Indians, and he established his home in Santiago de Baracoa, the first town in Cuba.

He raised cattle, sheep, and mares and was the first there to own a herd and a horse. He also mined gold with the help of Indian labor and was generally successful. Velasquez, now the governor of Cuba, was greatly impressed with him and entrusted him with many governmental affairs, Cortes working as the governor's secretary.

This relationship with the governor, Velasquez, however, was not always friendly. Cortes was reported to have joined with a group of conspirators against the governor. Velasquez heard of the plot and had him arrested, threatening to hang him. Many friends pled on Cortes' behalf, and he was pardoned and placed on a ship for deportation back to Spain. He escaped, however, and for a time took sanctuary in a local church (Cortes, l).

Following more threats and arguments accord was finally reached, and he was reprieved. Cortes was now married and comfortable in his home.

A NEW EXPEDITION

The governor, Velasquez, an eager opportunist, had followed closely the expeditions to the coasts beyond Cuba. Yucatan was discovered by Francisco Hernandez de Cordoba in 1517. The following year the governor sent his nephew, Grijalva, to this newly discovered land with two hundred Spaniards in four vessels to trade hoping to acquire much gold and silver.

Grijalva sailed to Cozumel, Yucatan, and continued along the coast to San Juan de Ulua, (near present-day Vera Cruz). He took possession of the land in the name of Velazquez for the King, traded his goods, and returned, but failed to start a colony.

Prior to Grijalva's return the governor, with further views of immense riches, proposed to Cortes that they be partners in an expedition, and since Grijalva was overdue, Cortes could be sent to find him. Cortes' energy and spirit were highly prized. He also had the courage and the desire, and he had accumulated a small amount of gold. He readily accepted the partnership. Eager to pursue the agreement, Cortes vigorously arranged for ships and provisions and recruited men to accompany him. In the meantime Grijalva had returned but Velasquez was so upset with his apparent failure he refused to see him.

During this preparation, enemies of Cortes seem to have once again bent Velasquez's ear, and the governor changed his mind. Cortes had been spending far too freely of the partnership funds, mostly provided by Velasquez. The governor also felt Cortes had a mind to take over the affair.

How could he trust Cortes, who was, after all, an Extremaduran (born of lowly station), crafty, haughty, touchy about his honor, and would seek vengeance for past wrongs?

Cortes refused to give up the previously planned expedition, borrowed money from other supporters, bought ships, horses and clothes, and rapidly organized for the venture. Reacting to this vigorous opposition, the governor ordered that no provisions should be given him and withdrew approval of the voyage—upon which Cortes determined to leave at once, going on his own authority, with the license of the governing Fathers.

Velasquez made one last attempt to stop him, begging him in letters to wait a little so that Velasquez could go with him, or send him word of certain important things. At the same time the governor had sent letters to Diego de Ordaz instructing him to arrest Cortes.

Ordaz invited Cortes to dine with him on board his ship thinking to take him captive to Santiago. But Cortes smelled a trap, pretended to have a stomachache, and didn't appear at dinner.

A final exchange of words is said to have been had between the governor and Cortes. Aware of his planned early departure Velazquez went to the harbor and called out after Cortes, "Why, compadre, is this the way you leave? Is this a fine way to say farewell to me?" From his heavily armed boat Cortes responded, "Forgive me, Your Worship, for this and similar things have to be done rather than thought about" (Cortes, 1). He departed from Baracoa on 18 November, 1518, with more than 300 Spaniards in six ships.

For several more weeks Cortes continued to gather ships, men, horses and provisions at other Cuban ports and from Trinidad and Jamaica. His attempt to get further provisions at Havana, Cuba, was partially stifled, however, for the people there were loyal to Velazquez and refused to sell to him, that is, except Cristobal de Queada, the Bishop's tithe collector, who sold him considerable salt, pork, maize, yucca, and chili.

Aboard his own flagship he set sail, hoisting his flag of white and blue flames with a cross in the middle on which the translated Latin motto read: "Friends, let us follow the cross, and with faith in this symbol we shall conquer." Even Diego de Ordaz, who had planned to capture him, joined and became one of his captains (Gomara, 7-21).

AZTEC MILITARY STRENGTH

The many kingdoms of Central America were militant societies. And the Aztec empire dominated this strongly militaristic region. Heroism in war brought rewards and glory to the warriors including rising from serfdom to the status of nobility.

The special war god of the Aztecs was Huitzilopochtli. Captured warriors were sacrificed to guarantee his continuing grace. Warriors who died in battle or on the sacrificial stone were declared to merit a special heaven. Conquering enemies included taking captives for sacrifice and burning in the local temple so that the Aztec god Huitzilopochtli, could be appeased and implanted in the conquered kingdom. Such basic practices and beliefs had created a very powerful, war oriented society.

Yet in a campaign that lasted less than nine months the Aztec empire had fallen and the Spaniards had triumphantly entered the capital city.

HOW WAS THE CONQUEST DONE?

In early February 1519, Cortes mustered his forces. They consisted of five hundred and eight soldiers, including thirty-two crossbowmen and thirteen musketeers, in addition to about one hundred sailors. They were provided with sixteen horses, ten cannons, and four lighter firing pieces called falconets. The men and equipment were transported in eleven vessels: one of a hundred tons and three of seventy tons, and the remainder smaller caravels and open brigantines (del Castillo, 42). They also had a good supply of amunition.

Sailing from Cuba Cortes made a short stop on the island of Cozumel. Among the most needed services was an interpreter. How could he conquer if he could not communicate? While on Cozumel he learned that the Spaniard Jeronimo de Aguilar would be adequately fluent in the language. Unfortunately he was somewhere in Yucatan and not easily reached. Cortes was impatient. He set forth from the port of Cozumel two or three times for New Spain (Mexico) but had to return on account of wild weather. This led him to believe that God wanted Aguilar and his companions brought back into his service. So Cortes sent Diego de Ordaz and Martin de Excalante as captains to lead them back to safety. Within a few days Aguilar was located and came from the mainland of Yucatan.

The story of de Aguilar fascinated Cortes and his crew. When Cortes asked him how he had come into the power of those Indians, Aguilar said,

> Being involved in the wars of Darien and the passions between Diego de Nicuesa and Blasco Nunez de Balboa, I accompanied Valdivia, who was going to Santo

Domingo to give an account of what was going on there to the admiral and governor and to get men and food as well as to bring twenty thousand ducats belonging to the king. This was the year 1511. And when we had already reached Jamaica, the caravel was lost on the shoals . . . of the vipers. With some difficulty twenty of us entered the small vessel, without sails and without bread or water and with very poor equipment of oars.

"And in this way we went on for fourteen days at the end of which the current, which is very strong there and always follows the sun, brought us to this land to a province called Maya. On the way seven of our men died of hunger, and the rest falling into the power of a cruel lord, he sacrificed Valdivia and four others, and, offering them to his idols, afterwards ate them, making a feast according to the custom of the country; and I, together with six others, remained in a coop, in order that for another festival that was approaching, being fatter, we might solemnize their banquet with our flesh. Understanding that the end of our days was drawing near, we decided to venture our lives in another way, so we broke the cage in which we had been placed, and, fleeing through the bush without being seen by a living person, God willed that although we went on with great fatigue, we should meet another cacique, an enemy of the one from whom we were fleeing. He was a humane and affable man, a friend of well doing. He was called Ah-kin Cuz (Aquincuz), governor of Jamancona. He granted us our lives, although in exchange for great servitude in which he placed us. He died a few days later and I then served Taxmar, who succeeded him in the state.

Five of my other companions died shortly thereafter on account of the miserable life they endured. I alone remained, and one sailor, Gonzalo Guerrero. . . . I believe he failed to come on account of . . . his love for his children (Landa, 236).

Aguilar was well acquainted with the Mayan language and served as a much needed interpreter for Cortes during the expedition. Cortes also acquired the services of other interpreters as the need arose.

From Cozumel, Cortes moved along the shore of Yucatan, skirmished with some 40,000 opposing Tebascans, and landed, April 21, 1519, in the vicinity of the present day city of Vera Cruz on the Gulf of Mexico.

AZTEC PERSPECTIVE ON THE COMING OF CORTES

For many years the Aztecs had been observing events for which no explanation could be given and which caused them great concern.

FLOODING OF MEXICO CITY BY LAKE TEXCOCO. In 1510, nine years before Cortes reached the shore of the mainland, Lake of Texcoco, the lake in which the island city of Tenochtitlan (Mexico City), Montezuma's capital, was located, overflowed its banks. The water foamed up, swirled, boiled up with a cracking sound. Water poured into the streets of the city sweeping off many buildings. It was as though a high tide had arisen, and yet Texcoco was not tidal. There had been no tempest, no earthquake or other visable cause (Sahagun, 12:2).

FIRE IN THE GREAT TEMPLE. The following year a fire broke out in the great temple of Huitzilopochtli, the war god, and continued to burn defying all efforts to extinguish it. No arsonist was known to have set it on fire, but it simply burst into flames. The wooden pillars were already burning when the fire was first seen. When water was thrown on to put it out it flared up all the more (Sahagun, 12:2).

A THREE-TAILED COMET. One day while it was yet light a comet arose from where the sun set and traveled toward the east. Its tail went a great distance and appeared to be sprinking live coals. The tail then separated into three tails that trailed along behind. At the same time a great noise was heard (Sahagun, 2).

A PYRAMID OF FIRE IN THE SKY. The sky also revealed another foreboding sign. Not long before the Spaniards arrived a strange light appeared in the east . It came at midnight making it appear that dawn had come, and it remained in the sky until the sun came up. It was like a tongue or sheet of fire, showering sparks like a flame. It was broad at the base on the horizon rising in the form of a pyramid at the zenith. This sign appeared for a full year. All who saw it were frightened and waited with dread. They cried out striking the palm of the hand against the mouth (Ibid., 1).

Gomara, Cortes' secretary and scribe, described this strange sight. He says that not long before Hernando Cortes came unto the new Spain, there appeared after midnight for many nights in a row a great lightning of fire, a flame of fire which seemed to touch the heavens. It appeared toward the east, at the same port where Cortes entered, where Vera Cruz is now located, causing great fear in the Mexicans (Gomara,294).

At the same time low voices were heard in the sky, wailings as though announcing some strange calamity. Often a woman was heard weeping, crying aloud at night, "My beloved sons. Now we are about to go!" She was thought to be the earth goddess (Dibble, 13).

A STRANGE BIRD WAS CAUGHT. On one occasion a group of hunters were snaring game and they caught an ashen hued bird like a brown crane. On its head was a round, circular mirror in which appeared the stars of heaven, the Fire Drill constellation. When Montezuma saw this he took it as an omen of great evil. As he looked at the bird's head a second time, he saw, a little beyond, what was like people coming massed, coming as conquerers, "girt in war array. Deer bare them upon their backs" (Sahagun, 12:3).

PROPHECY FROM THE DEAD. There was even one account

of the resurrection of Montezuma's sister, Papantzin, four days after her burial, warning the monarch of the approaching ruin of his empire (Prescott, 172).

AN ARMY IN THE SKY. Gomara related that the Indians also saw the figures of armed men fighting in the air one with another, a new and strange sight, and a thing that filled their heads with imaginations. There was an ancient prophecy among them, how that white men with beards should come and rule their kingdom in the time of Montezuma. The Lords of Texcoco and Tlacopan, two small local kingdoms, were much amazed, saying, that the sword which Montezuma had, was used as a weapon by this strange army, whose figures they had seen in the air, with their apparel and attire.

Montezuma tried to pacify them, saying that the weapon and apparel was of his forefathers. To convince them of this, he gave them his sword, and asked them to break it if they could. They tried but could not, marveling at its firmness, and seemed to accept Montezuma's explanation. Gomara concluded that whatever the reasoning the Lords were convinced that they would be ruined with the arrival of men dressed and armed as those seen in the sky.

A VISION TO ONE TO BE SACRIFICED. The very year in which Cortes arrived at Mexico, a malli (that is, a prisoner of war destined for sacrifice), who was bewailing his ill fortune and death, and calling upon God in heaven, saw a vision which told him not to fear death, because God, to whom he had commended himself, would have mercy on him; that he should tell the priests and ministers of the idols that sacrifice and the sprinkling of human blood would soon cease, because those who were to stop it and seize the country were at hand. They sacrificed him in [the square of] Tlatelolco, but his words and his vision (which they called a wind from heaven) were remembered (Gomara, 349; Cortes, 294-295).

WHAT DID ALL THESE OMENS MEAN? Montezuma was terrified and called for his chief astrologer who proved to be a prophet of doom. He interpreted these extraordinary things as omens or portents pointing toward the speedy downfall of the empire.

CORTES AND THE RETURN OF QUETZALCOATL

Ever present in Montezuma's mind was one other concern. It was the tradition of the return of Quetzalcoatl. Who was Quetzalcoatl, and why should Montezuma be so concerned? Quetzalcoatl was an ancient and revered god throughout Middle America, creator, god, priest, ruler, a god of learning and science. He was a god of many centuries ago, of fair complexion and flowing beard (Indians had no beard) who after filling his mission of teaching and benevolence left, promising to return at some future day and again be leader of the empire.

It was a day to which all looked forward with great confidence. He was a god of peace and love. There was a general feeling that the return of Quetzalcoatl was near at hand. The omens supported the feeling. Yet to Montezuma it would mean the end of his rule.

There was also special significance in the time of arrival of Cortes which bothered Montezuma. By tradition the god Quetzalcoatl had been born in the Aztec year One Reed, a recurring year designation. By the same version of tradition, One Reed was also the year of his departure to the east. The year 1519, the year of the Spaniards' arrival was in the Aztec calendaring the year One Reed.

There was further significance in the direction from which the Spaniards came. They came from the east, the same direction into which Quetzalcoatl was said to have departed and from which he would return.

A more detailed prophecy lay heavily on Montezuma's mind. Quetzalcoatl represented a peaceful theocratic society. When he left Tula as militarism took over he spoke to them at length. Thus Fray Diego Duran of the Dominican order, reared in Mexico in the 16th century, told of his conversation with a learned Indian. "He [Topiltzin (Quetzalcoatl)] prophesied the arrival of strangers who would come to this land from the east. They wore unusual and multicolored clothing from head to foot. They used head coverings. This was the punishment which God was to send them in return for the ill-treatment which Topiltzin had received and for the shame of his banishment. In this chastisement young and old were to perish. No one was to escape from the hands of his sons who were to come to destroy them. Even if the people hid in caves and in the caverns of the earth, from these they would be brought forth, they would be persecuted and slain" (Duran, 61-62).

He adds further, "I asked the Indian whether he knew or had heard where the priest had gone. Although he told me some incredible things, he confirmed my idea that Topiltzin had gone toward the seacoast. He was never heard from again, nor is it known where he went. The only thing known is that he went to inform the Spaniards, his sons, about this country and that he brought them for the sake of vengeance. So it is that the Indians, having been told of the ancient prophecy of the coming of strangers, were always anticipating it.

Thus when news came to Montezuma of the arrival of the Europeans at San Juan de Ulua and Coatzacualco, he already knew of their dress and their customs. Montezuma examined the ancient paintings and books and realized that they were the sons of Topiltzin, whose arrival had already been announced to him. So he sent them a splendid present consisting of jewels, feathers, gold, and precious stones. In fear of what had come upon him, [Montazuma] sent a message asking the newcomer to depart, since he did not wish to see him. He knew through his prophecies that the strangers had not come to bring good, but rather evil and harm" (Ibid., 68-69).

WHAT SHOULD MONTEZUMA DO?

With these many omens, portents, prophecies and traditions bearing on him what should Montezuma do? He was aware of the landing of the Spaniard Grijalva the previous year. Fearful of Grijalva's return or the approach of others, he had posted sentinels along the coast to warn him. When Montezuma received information of the arrival of the Spaniards in 1519 the following is reported: "He thought that this was Topiltzin (Quetzalcoatl) who had come to land. For it was in their hearts that he would come to land, just to find his mat, his seat. For he had traveled there [eastward] when he departed" (Sahagun, 12:9).

Thus Montezuma sent emissaries with the array of Quetzalcoatl to meet Cortes.

CORTES RECEIVED THE EMISSARIES OF MONTEZUMA

Shortly thereafter Cortes was visited by the local governor and messengers from Montezuma, emperor of the Aztecs, who came aboard the Spanish ship. Cortes was given gifts of fine cottons, mantles of curious feather-work and a basket of ornaments of wrought gold. In return he also presented gifts including some ornaments of cut glass, treasured by the Mexicans.

The emissaries addressed Cortes: "May the god deign to hear: his governor, Montezuma, who watcheth over Mexico for him, prayeth unto him. He sayeth: 'The god hath suffered fatigue, he is weary.'" Then they proceeded to dress Cortes in a most unusual way. They put on him a turquoise [mosaic] serpent mask with which went a quetzal feather head fan. They inserted green stone serpent earplugs. They also put on him a sleeveless jacket and a plaited green stone neck band in the midst of which lay a golden disc. About the calf of his leg they placed a green stone band with golden shells. On his arm they placed a shield with lines of gold and shells crossing, on whose lower rim were spread quetzal feathers and a quetzal feather flag. Before him they set obsidian sandals, with three additional sets of highly adorned clothing. Cortes was a willing participant in such an elegant greeting. Hardly could he understand that this was the array of the gods, the special array of Quetzalcoatl (Sahagun, 12:15).

When this had been done, Cortes said to them: "Are these perchance all your gifts, your greetings?" They answered:

"This is all with which we came, O our Lord." Then Cortes commanded that they be bound. Irons were fastened about their ankles and necks. To impress them Cortes' men shot off a cannon which caused the messengers to faint away. When they revived they were given food and drink and further discussion followed.

During this interview the local governor observed a Spanish soldier with a shining gilt helmet on his head. He commented that it reminded him of the one worn by the god Quetzalcoatl in Mexico, and desired that Montezuma, the emperor, should see it. Cortez gave the helmet to him requesting that it be returned filled with gold dust so that he could compare it with the quality of that in his own country.

Cortez also stated that he and his men were troubled with a disease of the heart, for which gold was the specific remedy (Prescott, 166). The governor with the emissaries withdrew taking with them many sketches made by his artists, of Cortes, his men and his ships (water houses), to show to Montezuma Cortes, of course, was pleased with this favorable reception. He knew nothing of the background which caused him to be so welcomed. Nevertheless, he graciously received the kindness and planned to continue to the capital city.

THE COURT OF MONTEZUMA [MOTECUHEUMA] AND THE RECEPTION OF CORTES

A detailed account in the court of Montezuma as to the arrival of Cortes as recorded by Torquemada in his book Indiana Monarchy noted and recorded by Lord Kingsborough is as follows.

When that Spanish general arrived on the coast of New Spain he was not only taken by the Mexicans for their Messiah, but actually received their adorations in that character, seated on a throne erected for the purpose on the deck of his ship. To this absurd belief of the Mexicans, Torquemada is inclined to attribute the rapid progress of the Spanish arms, as the necessary consequence of the general commotion into which their empire was thrown by the rumor, every where circulated, that the Messiah had come to take possession of the kingdom.

The relation of Torquemada follows (translated by Lord Kingsborough):

When Juan de Grijalva prosecuted the discovery which Francisco Hernandez de Cordova had commenced along the coasts of New Spain, he arrived with his fleet at San Juan de Ulua, as has already been said; and since it was a new thing to the people of the land to behold ships on the sea—for never had such a thing entered their imaginations—it caused them great surprise and fear, and they reported the fact to the governors and commanders stationed by the Emperor Motecuhcuma through the whole of that district. On hearing these tidings they all assembled, and agreed amongst each other to do with the intelligence to their lord Motecuhcuma, who held his court in this city of Mexico; and in order not to proceed on mere surmise to disturb the kingdom, and for more perfect information on the subject of their mission, they determined to see that miracle or prodigy which terrified and kept them in alarm and admiration.

They settled, therefore, that some of their number should go to the sea, and embarking in canoes, should carry with them refreshments of bread and fruit and other provisions, that, if they were men like themselves, they might tell them that they came to sell those things to them if they stood in need of them; but should this not be the case, that they might inform themselves what those vast masses were, and what they contained within them. The plan was accordingly executed; and some principal Indians, men of resolution, took the charge on themselves, and embarking in canoes, rowed towards the ships; when seeing on one of them the royal standard fanned by the breeze, and supposing that in that, as in his proper vessel, the captain of all the others was, they proceeded to it and came on board.

Those in the ship, when they beheld them approaching, stationed themselves so as to observe what they did: but the

Indians, who in the mean time had come alongside of them, made them a profound reverence, and gave them to understand by signs that their intentions were peaceable, and that they came to sell them provisions and articles of dress. Those on board inquired likewise by signs of what country they were, and what had brought them thither. They answered that they were Mexicans. Our countrymen replied by saying, "Since you are Mexicans, inform us of the name of your king."

They said that his name was Motecuhcuma; and on this quitted their canoes to come on board the ship, which they entered without any distrust, and displayed before them rich cotton dresses and some articles of provision which highly gratified our countrymen, who exchanged them with the Indians for blue and green and other colored beads, which appeared to them to be of a very fine quality and to exceed in value the dresses which they had brought with them.

The Indians having concluded their barter of these articles, and remaining a considerable portion of the day in the ship, motioned to withdraw; when the captain said to them, "Farewell; carry these stones to your lord Motecuhcuma, and tell him that we are unable now to see him, since we are on our return to our own country, but that we shall come back again and shall pay him a visit at his city of Mexico:" on which the Indians embarked in their canoes and reached the shore, where they immediately painted, as well as they were able, the ships and their rigging, the persons whom they had seen, their dress, their features and beards, and other particular objects which appeared to them new and strange.

They then set off directly for Mexico, traveling with the greatest expedition night and day without stopping to take rest, and soon arrived at that city, and proceeded to the palace, confiding to no one the news of which they were the bearers, since it was not customary to declare or make public the purport of state dispatches before the king had listened to them and was in possession of the facts. They desired the porters to notify to Motecuhcuma of their arrival, and that they had come in haste.

The king was informed by his attendants in waiting that the governors and commanders of the coasts of the North Sea awaited his pleasure and had come in great haste to see him. The king was both troubled and surprised, as he judged that the affair must needs be very urgent, since those whom he had stationed on guard in that district had come without permissions to see him; (neither was his surprise without just cause, since he had strong reasons to anticipate something untoward, from the prodigies which he had beheld, which prognosticated to him adversity and approaching ruin, so that he was continually haunted with the suspicions of the great misfortunes which he foreboded). He replied to the attendants,"Is it true that the captains of the sea-coast have all come in a body?" They again addressed him and said, "Please your Majesty, they are without; let them be summoned into your presence and see you." Montecuhcuma answered, "Tell them that they may come in, I must see them."

As soon as they had entered the apartment in which he was, they immediately prostrated themselves to the ground and kissed it, and rising saluted the king, and said, "Lord, we are worthy of death for having come without your leave into your royal presence, but the nature of the business which has brought us is so grave and important that it must plead our excuse.

It is an undoubted truth that we all of us who have come here have seen gods, who have arrived on this coast in large water houses" (by this term they meant a ship), "and we have spoken, and conversed, and eaten with them, and given them rich mantles; and they have in return given us these precious stones which we have brought with us."

They then presented to him the beads and bugles which they had brought; and said, "They gave us these beads," and added, "Go to your court and give them to Motecuhcuma your Lord, and tell him that we are on our return to our own country, but shall come back again and pay him a visit." To this speech the emperor answered not a word, revolving the matter in his breast; but he simply observed to the captains, "You must feel weary after such a long and speedy journey; go and repose yourselves, and let not a word transpire of the intelligence which you have brought me; I wish it to be kept secret, lest it should cause commotion amongst the fickle and easily-excited populace." The captains withdrew, and they assigned to them the apartments which they were to occupy, since that was an ancient custom.

Motecuhcuma remained alone, pensive, and even very apprehensive of some great change in his kingdoms; for he was possessed of much foresight, and reflected on past prodigies which had happened, and recollected what his soothsayer had told him; in recompense for which he caused his house, while he was in it, to be thrown to the ground, and overwhelmed him in the ruins. He also called to mind what his sister Papan had informed him many years before, and what Necahualpilli had likewise said to him; and it appeared to him that these were not fortuitous coincidences, but that they portended some great disaster and change in the government: and since weighty matters of state are wont to be imparted to others and to be debated in council, he immediately caused summonses to be sent to all the persons of whom his council was composed, who were King Cacama of Tezcuco, his nephew, whom he sent for by express; Cuitlahuatzin, his brother, the lord of Itxtapalapan; Ycihuzcohuatl, Tlilpotonqui, Tlacochcalcatl, Quapiatzin, Tizoc, Yaoacatl, Quetzal-aztatzin, Huitzna-huacatl, Tlaylotlac, and Ecatempatilzin, who were his ordinary counselors; to whom he declared what had happened.

And a considerable time having been employed in the interchange of opinions and conjectures respecting the true state of the case, his council terminated their deliberations by persuading themselves and being convinced that it was Quetzalcohuatl, whom in times past they had worshiped as a god, and who they likewise expected would again return to reign over their kingdoms; since he himself had long before promised them that he would do so, when he departed from thence to the provinces of Tlapala and disappeared on the coast of the sea, going in the direction of the east; and since they on this account expected him, they thought that those who had arrived were his train.

Under this persuasion they resolved that a certain number of persons should be named to go and receive him: and whilst preparations were making in the mean time for their departure, orders were issued to the commanders and governors of the sea-coasts to be very vigilant in keeping a watch and look-out for every arrival by sea, especially on the coasts of Nauhtla, Toztla, Mictla, and Quahtla; since from those places, as being more conveniently situated, a better look-out could be kept and more speedy and certain intelligence brought to the court of any new event. With these commands the governors and commanders were dismissed, and five lords were appointed as bearers of the present which the emperor sent to Quetzalcohuatl, who were Yohualychan who was the principal, Tepuztecal who was nearly of equal rank, Tizahua and Huehuetecatl; the fifth and last was named Hueycamecatleca.

They were commanded to proceed as expeditiously as possible to the sea-coast, and to speak on the part of Motecuhcuma and of his senate to Quetzalcohuatl their lord, and to offer him the kingdom, and a rich present which was given to them that they might be the bearers of it. And this it was that Gomara and Antonio de Herrera make confused mention of, as having been brought to Ferdinand Cortes by the governors of Motecuhcuma on his first landing, which they notice in the following words: `Which present it is said was sent for Juan de Grijalva, when he touched on those shores; but that, notwithstanding the haste of those who carried it, they found he was gone.'

The fact was as they state; but I do not understand how those who drew up the account of which Herrera availed himself, should have omitted that which I say in this chapter, and many other particulars which shall be observed in the sequel;

since the circumstances which they mention, and those which I relate, are intimately connected with each other, and those who could have given an account of the former, could likewise have done so of the latter; although I think that the error lay in their only seeking information from the Spaniards, who at that period returned from the Indies, without verifying facts by applying to the Indians, who were mainly concerned in most of them, or I may say in all since they were the mark which all who have written on the affairs of the conquest strove to hit, and were those who were very well acquainted with them, and in the beginning recorded them by means of figures and characters, and afterwards, when some of the most curious amongst them had learned how to write, wrote them down; which histories are in my possession: and so high is the estimation in which I hold them, on account of their language and the style of their composition, that I should be glad to feel myself competent to the task of translating them into Spanish with the same elegance and grace as the Mexicans penned them in their own language; and since these histories are true and authentic, I follow them to the letter; but lest the accounts which they contain should appear strange to those who read them, I affirm that they are merely a true relation of what actually happened, but that other authors have not noticed them before me, because the few that have written on the affairs of the Indies were ignorant of the events which then occurred, nor had they any one to give them the requisite information; neither should I have mentioned these facts, had I not found that they were verified by Father Bernard de Sahagun, a grave and pious ecclesiastic, who was of the second number of those who undertook the conversion of the natives of New Sapin, but was the first of the investigators of the most secret things of this land, of which he knew all the secrets, and employed himself for more that sixty years in composing works in the Mexican Language, and in incorporation into it all the information which he was about to acquire . . .

In ancient times there was a man of the kingdom of Tula who was named Quetzalcohuatl, as we have observed elsewhere, who was a famous magician and necromancer, whom they afterwards worshiped as a god, and who was accounted a king of that country. He was conquered by another greater and more powerful magician, such another as we may suppose Zoroaster of Babylon to have been, who deprived him of his kingdom; from thence he fled to the city of Chollula, wither the other pursued him; when, forsaking that kingdom, he fled to the sea, pretending that the god, who was the sun, called him to the other side of the sea, to the borders of the East; but he promised that he would again return with great power to avenge himself of his enemies, and to redeem his people from their afflictions and the yoke of tyranny under which they groaned; for they said of him that he was very compassionate and merciful: this lie was preserved in the recollection of those who lived in that age, and acquired much greater credit in all the ages which afterwards succeeded; and the Mexicans so fully believed in his return, that their kings when mounting the throne, took possession of the kingdom upon the express condition of being vicars of their lord Quetzalcohuatl, and of abdicating it on his arrival, and obeying him in it as his vassals.

This history, therefore, being duly known, we assert that that nation expected Quetzalcohuatl, and believed it as very certain that he would return to rule over the kingdoms of New Spain; and on every symptom and demonstration of a change or rumor of any novelty, they immediately thought that it was he: and when they received the intelligence which we have mentioned in the preceding chapter, and further heard that they (The Spaniards) had arrived in the quarter where he had disappeared, and that they had come in large ships through the midst of so vast and dangerous an ocean, they felt convinced that it was he, and could be no one else: and for this reason they were still more vigilant in watching his return; placing sentinels to keep a look-out towards the sea—not for three days only during every month of the year, like the Gentiles of the East, but night and day the entire year round; at the expiration of which period, Juan de Grijalva having sailed to Cuba, and the expedi-

tion of Ferdinand Cortes by the same route, being the consequence of his return, it necessarily followed that the Indians
saw his ships, and, in obedience to the express commands of
their king, they proceeded post to carry him the intelligence,
taking with them paintings, in which were represented the
number of the vessels, and the kind of people whom they
beheld on board; all of which they showed to Motecuhcuma,
who, on receiving the news of this second armament (which
was towards the latter end of February of the year 1519) assembled those who constituted his council, and other persons possessed of talents and authority, and communicated to them the
tidings which had been brought to him by the sentinels of the
eastern sea-coast, of what had newly appeared on the sea,
which confirmed the accounts of the preceding year; and the
matter having been laid before them, they deliberated upon the
measures which it might be proper to adopt; and as, when the
Magi entered Jerusalem inquiring for the newly-born king,
Herod and all his confederates and partisans were troubled,
and the doctors consulted together and decided upon the place
where he should be born—so the Indians who composed the
council of the king were troubled together with him, and in
great perplexity replied, 'that since it was true that their god
and king Quetzalcohuatl had gone to the kingdom of Tlapala to
visit the god who was the sun, whose return all their forefathers
had expected, he likewise who had appeared in the ships might
be that god, since it was not humanly probable that mortal men
could have penetrated so far into the depths of the ocean without being swallowed up by its waves; and that therefore they
believed that it was he, and that, since he had come, it was fit
that ambassadors and noblemen should be sent to offer him
obedience upon the part of the senate, and to receive him.'
Hence, as we may infer, originated the custom amongst the
Mexicans of the monarchy being elective and not hereditary,
which we may prove by observing, that if they believed that they
had a living king, who at some time or other was to return to
take possession of his kingdom, it was impossible that they

could consent that another should enter upon the perpetual possession of it, but only that he should hold it like a viceroy, who in the absence of a king exercises all the regal functions, with a condition which implies that the exercise of those functions will be for no longer a period than during the absence of the latter, and that he will be ready and prepared to forgo them when and as soon as the natural and lawful heir should appear. But this was folly in them, as was also their believing that that magician had gone to visit the sun, in order afterwards to return to enjoy the earthly kingdom which he had forsaken: but I can well imagine that, granted that the devil had intended this piece of fraud, and devised this trick in order to deceive this nation, it was likewise by permission of God, not for the sake of keeping these mistaken men in a state of delusion, but in order that as soon as Christians should arrive in those parts with the annunciation and tidings of his Holy Gospel, they might be already in some measure disposed to receive it, from the warning which had been given to them, and the anxiety which they felt about another's coming and depriving them of the kingdom. But if the devil had been able thoroughly to comprehend the matter, he would have known that Quetzalcohuatl, whom he pretended to be the king and god of that nation, would in reality be the true God and Lord of the whole creation; and that, in the same manner as Cortes came to strip Motecuhcuma of the possession of his kingdom (whom the Indians, unconscious of the meaning of their message, sent to welcome as Quetzalcohuatl) so likewise that this lord and supreme king would come in the character of the monarch of the universe to destroy him, and to dispossess him of the kingdom, especially as they already had had forebodings of the same; it having been predicted to them ten years before by Papan the princess of Tlatelolco, as we read in a preceding book in the chapter which treats of the prodigies which portended the destruction of the Mexican empire.

Returning to my subject—I say that those Indians, having arranged with their king what under such peculiar circumstances ought to be done, prepared a great present (whether it might have been the same as that which had been sent for Juan de Grijalva and which had been brought back, or whether it was another like it, or a larger than the first, I do not know); but one addition which it received was, that they sent with it all the sacerdotal habits which they said had been worn by Quetzalcohuatl when he was in that country, who, as it would hence appear, was both priest and king, like Numa Pompilius in Rome: and here we have an example of the pontifical and regal dignities having been united at one period of time in the world, as we have elsewhere observed. All the articles of which the present consisted, Motecuhcuma took from his treasury in order that they might be sent to those strangers who had made their appearance by sea, where wrapped up in rich mantles which they put into petacas, which having been done, Motecuhcuma made the following speech to the lords whom he sent as his ambassadors: "Go, my friends, and discharge faithfully the duties of this embassy, which we entrust to you, this august senate and myself; take care that nothing detains you on the road, but proceed with as much expedition as possible into the presence of our lord and king Quetzalcohuatl, and say to him, `Your vassal, Motecuh-cuma, who is at present the regent of your kingdom, sends us to salute your majesty, and to give you the present of which we are the bearers, together with these sacerdotal ornaments, which have always been held in the highest veneration and esteem amongst us.' Charged with this dispatch, the ambassadors withdrew from the presence of the king, and immediately set out on their journey; and traveling with the greatest possible haste arrived at the sea-coast, which Cortes with his entire company had already reached.

On their coming to the sea-coast they embarked in canoes, into which they conveyed all their baggage, and directed their course to the ships of Ferdinand Cortes; and perceiving the flag of the captain's vessel, they rowed towards it, imagining that there they should find the lord and king whom they sought. All on board the ships intently observed what passed, and when the canoes reached the captain's vessel, the Indians gave them to understand by signs that they wished to come on board; those on deck inquired of them whence they came, who they were, and what they wanted; they replied that they were Mexicans, and that they had quitted Mexico to seek their lord and king Quetzalcohuatl, who they knew was there. Although the Spaniards did not understand their words, they knew the purport of them by their signs and, astonished at their demand, they debated the matter with each other, and said, `What can they mean by saying that their king and their god is here, and that they wish to see him? Cortes listened to their conversation, and he and all the rest having considered the matter well and deliberated together, they agreed amongst each other that Don Ferdinand Cortes should dress himself in the richest apparel that he had, and that they should prepare a throne for him in the fore part of the vessel, on which he should sit counterfeiting royalty, and that the Indians should then be introduced to see and speak to him. Having accordingly so done; they told the Indians that they were welcome, and that he whom they sought was there, and that they would be permitted to see and speak to him. The Indians on hearing this drew their canoes closer to the captain's vessel, and those above assisted them, and lifted up the baggage which they had brought with them: they as soon as they found themselves in the ship sat down on the deck, and dressed and adorned themselves with their finest ornaments, and untying their packages disposed the articles of which the present consisted in judicious order. Have so done, they begged to be permitted to behold him whom they sought: and were conducted to the fore part of the vessel, where Ferdinand Cortes was already expecting them, with the mock majesty which we have just mentioned: they were introduced to him carrying the present in their hands; and when they saw him seated majestically on the throne, believing that he was their god and lord Quetzalcohuatl, they immediately prostrated themselves upon the ground and kissed it—that being the obsequious mark of adoration with which they did homage to their gods; when, rising he who was the principal of them all, addressed him, `Our God and Lord, we welcome your arrival, since we, who are your vassals and servants, have long expected you. Motecuhcuma, your vassal and the regent of your kingdom, has dispatched us to your presence that we may salute you in his name, and he beseeches you to accept this trifling present, and these precious ornaments which you were accustomed to wear when you were amongst us in the character of our king and god.' Having so said, they began to attire him in the ornaments which they had brought; upon his head they put what seemed like a helmet decorated with gold and gems and great value and with a rich plume of feathers; they clothed him in a vest of the fine texture, named a Xiculli, which reached from the throat to the waist, and descended to the middle of the arm; they next threw a chain of precious stones of great value and beauty round his neck: and in this manner they proceeded to load him from head to foot with ornaments and costly sacerdotal vestments, adding to the ordinary habits worn by the god Quetzalcohuatl those likewise which belonged to the gods Tezcatlipoca and Tlalocatecutli, all of which they laid at his feet (as is also customary with them when they make a present to a person of high rank) signifying by that act that they recognized him as the greatest of their gods. After they had so done, an interpreter said to them in the name of Ferdinand Cortes, `What! Is this all that you have brought me to welcome my arrival amongst you:' On which the principal ambassador replied, `Lord and king! This was what was given to us to carry to your majesty, and no more.' Ferdinand Cortes then desired some of his men to take them into the cabin and to treat them courteously allowing them time to repose themselves, and afterwards to set before them provisions of Spain, inviting them to partake of them with all civility and politeness. When these Indians came on board the ship, many of the men crowded from the other vessels around the captain's ship to see what was there passing; and they saw and heard what I have related: at which they were astonished, and were at a loss for suitable terms by which to express what they thought of such great simplicity and of a scene so new to them.

They agreed to terrify these messengers by throwing them into irons, loading them with chains, and discharging the artillery, and challenging them to wrestle with them; all with the object of inducing them to report terrible things of them in order that those who heard them might be seized with fear, and dread them as those who were fated to march on to victory, and to become the lords of the country. The Indians slept in the ship that night, and on the next day as soon as it was morning the Spaniards put into execution what they had planned the day before: they took the Indians and threw them into irons, and having chained them by the feet began to fire off artillery.

The Indians, who beheld themselves prisoners and in irons, confounded with the noise and the thunders of the cannon and the smell of the powder, fell senseless on the ground, and there remained for a long space of time as if were dead: the soldiers, on seeing them in this state, raised them in their arms, and seating them, threw water in their faces, and made them drink it; on which they recovered from the terror and fright into which they had been thrown. They then took off their fetters; and the captain said to them, `I am informed that the Mexicans are very valiant, possess great strength, and are good wrestlers, and that one alone would be enough to conquer ten or twenty of his enemies, and to compel them to submit; on which account, in order to ascertain the truth and to assure myself of the fact, I wish you to contend with my people, that I may see whether you are more valiant than they.' He gave them shields, swords, and lances for the contest. The poor unhappy Indians, who, if even they had known how to make use of the arms which had been given to them, were more dead than alive from the chains and the noise of the artillery, did not only not accept the challenge, but declined it by saying, `Lord! This was not the purpose for which we came, nor did

Motecucuma send as to quarrel with you, or to enter upon a trial of strength with your people, but only to visit you in his name, and to kiss your hands as we have done; and if we obeyed your commands, and could be guilty of such great presumption, we should not only excite his displeasure, but should pay the forfeit of our lives.'

To this the captain replied, 'You need make no manner of excuse, for you must do what I order you; as I have heard of you Mexicans that you are valiant, and you must use your utmost endeavors in attacking and defending yourselves from my men.' He could not however prevail upon them; and seeing that they would not either singly, or two and two, or in any way try their strength and skill in fighting with the Spaniards, in order to induce them to accept the challenge, they loaded them with abusive epithets and dismissed them, telling them that they were cowards and effeminate persons, and that being such they might go back to Mexico, and that they would come and conquer the Mexicans, who should all die by their hands; and that they might tell Motecuhcuma that his present had displeased them, and that they would march to Mexico and would plunder them of whatever they had and take it for themselves. (Whether they knew what they were saying or not will be seen in the sequel; for they spoke at random, not knowing the future, and without having made any trial of the land.)

With this answer and these threats (worthy most certainly of the folly of Motecuhcuma and of his counselors) the Indians entered into their canoes; and so great was their haste that every moment's delay appeared to them the herald and harbinger of death: they immediately therefore began rowing—not only the rowers whom they had brought for the purpose, but all indiscriminately, each urging and exhorting the other to apply a strong hand to the oar, as well in order to find themselves at a distance from and fairly rid of the ships where they had been treated so indifferently, as to hasten their return, to give an account to their king of what had passed between them and Quetzalcohuatl. Proceeding in this rapid manner, they reached a small island called Xicalanco, where they partook of some refreshment and rested themselves for a short space of time; from thence, continuing their course, they arrived at a town named Tecpantlayacac on the sea-coast, from whence they journeyed on to Cuetlaxtla, a place situated some leagues inland, where they slept; the lords and principal persons of that town entreated them to remain there the following day to rest themselves; but they replied, `Our haste is urgent; for the embassy with which we are charged to our lord Motecuhcuma is of such a nature that it is unprecedented in these kingdoms, and it is not fit that any one should know its nature before him; and for this reason it is our duty not to stay to repose ourselves, but to travel on in haste.' They immediately set off, and proceeded on their journey with such distressed and harassed feelings, that they reaped no consolation from food or sleep, nothing gave them the slightest satisfaction, but they sighed as they went along, overcome with sorrow, wonder, and dismay; they scarcely addressed each other, preserving a strange silence; or if at intervals they spoke, they said, `We have beheld terrible and uncommon things, which portend evils and great tribulation; but, O Lord God! Who are they, and from whence shall they come, who shall conquer the Mexicans? Are not we the powerful, the ancient, and the dreaded in all these lands? Why do we allow ourselves to be disturbed and pained? Why do our hearts, heaving within our breasts forbode to us future ills?—this is a sign of some great impending calamity.' With these and similar reflections they occupied their minds on the road, and arrived by rapid stages at the city of Mexico at an advanced hour of the night, and proceeded straight to the palace of king Motecuhcuma, when they bade the attendants in the ante-room inform the king of their arrival; and if he was asleep to awaken him, for the business upon which they came did not permit delay or procrastination, and to say to him, `Lord! The ambassadors have returned whom you sent to the sea to receive our god Quetzalcohuatl' The guards went into his chamber and delivered the message to him, which when Motecuhcuma had heard, he answered, 'Tell them not to come in here, but to go to the hall of judgment, and to wait for me there.' He then commanded slaves to be prepared for a sacrifice, and proceeding to the hall of judgment, he assembled those who composed his council, and other persons whose office it was to sacrifice the slaves, with whose blood they sprinkled the ambassadors. This was a customary ceremony on the arrival of any very important embassy, when the circumstances which gave rise to it were grave and unusual.

After the idolatrous ceremony of sprinkling the ambassadors with the blood of these sacrificed victims had been gone through, Motecuhcuma seated himself upon his throne and chair, in order to hear with state and majesty the tidings which his ambassadors had brought to him: for agreeably to the belief which he had adopted, he was convinced that it was Quetzalcohuatl who had arrived on the sea-coast; and he expected to receive perfect information of the arrangements necessary to be made preparatory to his visit. The ambassadors immediately prostrated themselves upon the ground and kissed it (which they name in their language Tlalcualiztli, being an idolatrous ceremony of adoration) and in this prostrate state, the principal person amongst them, who had gone as superior of the rest of that embassy, commenced the delivery of the following speech: 'Powerful lord and king! As soon as we arrived at the sea shore, these your servants and myself, we beheld some very large houses entirely of wood upon the water, contrived very artificially both within and without, which go through the deep water of the sea like the canoes which we employ here upon our lake and aqueducts: we were told that these houses were called ships; and it would be impossible for any of us to explain the variety of buildings and things which they contain within them. We went in canoes to them, and entered the principal ship, or water-house, where was the flag which they carried with them. The ships were many; and in each there were many persons, who all stood looking at us until we entered the captain's vessel. We immediately requested to see the lord Quetzalcohuatl (in search of whom we had come) in order to give him the presents which we had brought with us: and they showed us, in a separate part of the ship, a lord seated upon a throne, clothed in very rich apparel, and pointing to him with their finger, they said to us, `Behold him whom you seek.' We prostrated ourselves at his feet, kissing the ground and adoring him as a god. We next addressed the speech to him which you commanded, and proceeded to dress him in the robes and jewels which you gave to us, and delivered to him the other articles of which the present consisted: and having laid it all at his feet, he gave us to understand that it was very little. That day they treated us well, and set provisions before us, and gave us an agreeable liquor to drink, which they called wine: that night we slept in the ship. In the morning they wished us to come to a trial of strength with us, and ordered us to fight with them, which we persisted steadily in declining: they then threw us into chains and discharged their artillery, which greatly terrified us with thunder and lightning, and caused us to fall on the ground as if dead. After we had recovered ourselves, and they had obliged us to take some refreshment, we inspected their arms, their horses, and their dogs which assist them in fighting, at which we were still more terrified. It would be tedious and would take up too much time to give a minute account of every thing which we saw:—they say that they have come here to conquer us and to rob us; that is all we know. If they should come here, we shall know both what they want, and how far their power may be commensurate with their will. We can only say that we return back greatly terrified and alarmed.'—Montecuhcuma was very much astonished at the words of the ambassadors; his face changed color, and he displayed extreme sorrow and dismay; the conviction took possession of his mind, that he himself was well as all the subjects of his empire would have to suffer much and to endure many indignities. Under the influence of this impression he began to weep bitterly, as did likewise all those by whom he was surrounded: their tears and lamentations spread afterwards through all classes of the city high and low; and they soon began to assemble in groups in the public squares and the streets, and to utter lamentations, each one exciting the other's grief by the suggestion of melancholy and tender recollections: they spoke of the great evils which threatened them and of the ruin and destruction which impended over them, as if they had already happened—their hearts divining what was afterwards to befall them: all were dejected and a prey to grief; fathers sorrowing for their sons exclaimed, `Alas, my sons, what troubles must you see, and, what is worse, what must you go through and suffer!' Mothers made the same lamentations over their daughters; adding other piteous ejaculations, which their great love and sorrow prompted. They passed the night and an entire day in their manifestations of public affliction; and Motecuhcuma, as more interested in preserving the honors and dignities which it might be his fate to lose, felt more acutely than all the rest" (Kingsborough, VI:338 -345).

With the Spaniards now at the Mexican shore let us observe the preparations made for Cortes' arrival among the Mexicans, the Aztecs.

RETURN OF THE MESSENGERS
AFTER GREETING CORTES

When these messengers returned to Montezuma after greeting Cortes he could neither sleep nor eat. He became weak. Nothing brought him contentment or brought him out of his depression. He was even more frightened when he heard how the cannon discharged."It resounded like thunder when it went off. It overpowered one; it deafened our ears. And when it discharged, something like a round pellet came forth from within. Fire scattered forth; sparks showered forth. And its smoke smelled very foul; it had a fetid odor which, verily, wounded the head. And when [the pellet] struck [a] mountain, [it was] as if it fell apart and crumbled. And when it struck a tree, it splintered, seeming to vanish as if someone blew it away" (Sahagun, 12:19).

Montezuma bemoaned: "What will befall us now? Who indeed standeth [in command]? Alas, until now, I. In great torment is my heart; as if it were washed in chili water, it indeed burneth, it smarteth. Where in truth [may we go], O our Lord?" (Sahagun, 12:17, 18).

CAPTIVES SACRIFICED AND BLOODED FOOD SENT TO CORTES

Without noting the receipt of an answer to his question Montezuma went to Coacalli and had two captives sacrificed; their breasts were cut open and blood was sprinkled on the messengers. "For this reason did they do so, that they had gone to very perilous places; that they had gone to see, to look into the faces, the heads of the gods—had verily spoken to them" (Sahagun, 12:17-18).

Montezuma then gathered food for the Spaniards, turkey, eggs, white tortillas, all they might desire. With the food he sent captives to be sacrificed since the Spaniards may want to drink their blood. In fact the food had been soaked in blood, covered with blood, reeked of blood, all of which nauseated the Spaniards. Still Montezuma was only so acting because he thought them to be gods, he worshiped them as gods. They were called "gods come from the heavens" (Ibid., 21).

CORTES MOVES TOWARD MEXICO CITY

As Cortes approached the capital city he came in conflict with various small kingdoms. The nature of the conflict caused Montezuma great concern. This concern arose over the Spanish attitude and approach to these conflicts. To Montezuma war and victory were considered to be a manifestation of the will of the gods and not that of military might. When those of one kingdom were to attack another they warned the enemy, even provided arms. Then they sought the guidance of magicians and soothsayers prior to and during the battle.

Thus as Cortes moved toward the city of Tenochititlan (Mexico City, the royal capital) Montezuma sought the aid of helpers numerous times to dissuade the Spaniards (Dibble, 19).

The soothsayers and magicians were sent "that they might behold what kind [of men] they were, use their wizardry upon them, cast a spell over them . . . perhaps they might blow them away, or enchant them, . . . cast stones at them, or they might, with some words of the Evil One, utter an incantation over them, so that they might take sick, die, or else because of it turn back" (Sahagun, 12:22). But they found they had no power over the Spaniards. They reported to Montezuma: "We cannot contend against them; we are as nothing" (Sahagun, 12:22).

"When Montezuma saw that the sorcerers had been unable to harm the Spaniards he tried to strengthen his spirit for he was more determined than ever not to allow the Spaniards to enter Mexico. He decided to put obstacles in their way and he could have done this easily had not God blinded his reason, whereupon the Divine Will was fulfilled" (Duran, 277-278).

CANNONS AND HORSES

As historians have observed the conquest many attribute Cortes' success for the most part to superior equipment. No doubt the ten cannons, four falconets (light firing pieces), ammunition, cross bows, and sixteen horses brought great advantage. These evoked fear and wonderment in the Indians, as well as provided means for extensive destruction of property and mass killing of any opponents.

In addition the Spaniards made war by different methods and motives from the Aztecs. To the Indians war was a seasonal activity. There was a time to plant, a time to harvest and a time to fight. After the harvest was done in late November and early December it was time to wage war. Boundaries were reestablished, borders were defended, treaties were broken, great losses were suffered, cities were plundered, captives and slaves were taken and many died. "Cities were seized, provinces conquered in order that each might extend his kingdom and dominion. And before the harvest none of this was customary lest the maize and the fields be laid waste and destroyed" (Torquemada, 299).

Cortes arrived at the port of San Juan de Ulua on April 21, 1519. For the next eight months they moved through various cities on the way to Tenochtitlan (Mexico City). They entered the city on Nov. 8, 1519. The entire march was made during a period of limited or nonexistent military activity in the regular order of Aztec life. It was during the period of planting and harvesting (Dibble, 25).

The chief reason for fighting among the natives was to take captives who would be sacrificed later to the gods. A successful battle was one in which the victorious warrior drug off his captive by the hair. In the battle with the Spaniards at Mexico City, the Aztecs captured Spanish soldiers, horses and natives who had joined as allies with Cortes. The Aztecs promptly sacrificed their victims stringing their heads on a skull rack (even the horses' heads) (Dibble, 25). "A war in which one camp (the Spaniards) was seeking to annihilate the contending camp (the Aztecs) was not within the understanding or concept of war among the Aztecs.

ENTRY INTO MEXICO CITY

These background events laid a foundation for the successful entry of the Spaniards into Mexico City. Bernal Dias Castillo, a soldier who accompanied Cortes, reported the situation of the presence of the Spaniards in the court of Montezuma. "Now that he (Montezuma) had us with him, he was ready to serve us and give all that he had, for truly we must be those of whom his ancestors had spoken long ago when they said that men would come from where the sun rises to be lords over these lands." (Chronicles, page 145.)

MONTEZUMA EXPLAINED HIS FEELINGS OF THE GOD TO COME

Andres de Tapia, another who accompanied Cortes, recorded an incident. In reference to some gold objects which were taken by Cortes' soldiers without permission. Montezuma is reported to have said to Cortes: "That belongs to the gods of our people. Leave the things like plumes and other pieces that are not gold, and take the gold. I shall give you all that I have. For you must know that from time immemorial my ancestors believe that a people from whom we all descend came to this land from very far, and they came in ships, then went away again leaving the land populated. They said they would return, and we have always believed that some time they would come to rule and command us. Our gods and diviners have always affirmed it, and I think that now it is fulfilled. I regard you as our lord and thus shall I have all my vassals and subjects regard you."

They shed many tears, saying: "It seems that in our time the fates wished to see fulfilled what so long was prophesied." (*The Conquistadors*, 39,40)

It wasn't long, however, before grounds for doubt as to such divinity of Cortes and his men began to be seen.

The Spaniards had entered the capital city without serious conflict. Once there and established in quarters they began to ransack the treasure houses. The most treasured possessions were destroyed or stolen. The finest works of highly skilled artisans in quetzal feathers were burned. Gold attached to shields and other devices was torn off and the remains burned. The Aztecs wondered how anyone who would burn precious feathers could be divine. Doubt and confusion first crept into them which soon reigned heavily in their minds.

What caused Montezuma to be so fearful, to have such deep feelings that Cortes was a returning god?

We shall now examine a few of the writers who present the background that led Montezuma to feel the way he did—first the native writers, then the historians, followed by Spanish conquistadors, priests, and other observers, finally an appendix.

Centuries earlier was the appearance of a man in mid-America among the natives called Quetzalcoatl A native writer related concerning him.

Fernando de Alva Ixtlilxochitl
(abt. 1578 – 1650)

Ixtlilxochitl, a native born scholar of Mexico, is considered by many to be the most prolific early writer on the history of Mexico. His place of birth was Texcoco, a present suburb of Mexico City. His date of birth is estimated to have been in 1568. He died in 1650. He was a descendant of Mexican royalty being a descendant of the last king of Texcoco. He was also of Spanish descent as his grandfather on his mother's side was the Spaniard Juan Grande.

PROLOGUE TO THE READER

Considering the variety and contrary opinions of the authors who have discussed the histories of this New Spain, I haven't wanted to follow any of them; and so I took advantage of the paintings and characters that are those with which their histories are written and memorized, because of having painted at the time and when the things occurring actually happened, and of the songs with which they observed them, very serious authors in a manner of science and faculty; for they were the very kings and the most illustrious and learned of the people, who always observed and acquired the truth, and this with so much calculation and reason, as much as the most serious and reliable authors and historians of the world could have; because they had their writers for each genre, some who dealt with the annals, putting in the proper order the things that happened in each year, with the day, month, and hour. Others had charge of the genealogies and lineages of the kings and lords and persons of lineage, carefully stating those who were born, and with the same care they would cross out those who died. Some had care of the paintings of the areas, limits, and boundary markers of the cities, provinces, towns, and places, and of the lots and distribution of the lands, whose they were and to whom they belonged. Others, of the books of the laws, rites, and ceremonies that they used in their infidelity; and the priests, of the temples, of their idolatries and manner of their idolatrous doctrine and of the festivals of their false gods and calendars. And finally, the philosophers and wise men that they had among them, who had the charge of painting all the sciences that they knew and understood, and teaching from memory all the songs that observed their sciences and histories; all of which changed the time with the fall of the kings and lords, and [with] the works and persecutions of their descendants and the calamity of their subjects and vassals. Not only was what was good and not contrary to our holy Catholic faith not pursued, but the largest part of them was burned unwittingly and inconsiderately by the order of the first religious persons, which was one of the greatest damages that this New Spain had; because in the city of Tetzcuco were the royal archives of all the things mentioned, because of its having been the metropolis of all the sciences, uses, and good customs, because the kings that had existed of that city prided themselves on this and they were the legislators of this new world; and some of what escaped the fires and calamities mentioned, which my elders kept, came into my hands, from where I have taken and translated the history that I am promising, although at the present in a brief and summary narration, achieved with much work and diligence in understanding the interpretation and knowledge of the paintings and characters that were their letters, and the translation of the songs in understanding their true meaning; which will go out succinct and flat, without adornment or help from examples; nor will I deal with the fables and fictions that appear in some of their histories, because they are superfluous things. And so I very lovingly ask the discrete reader to overlook the many defects that there may be in my manner of narrating, for you can be sure that that which is the history is very reliable and true, and approved as such by all the principal and illustrious people of this New Spain (Ixtlilxochitl I:527, 528).

SUMMARY

Summary narration of the general history of this New Spain from the origin of the world until his present era— gathered and taken from the histories, paintings, and characters of its natives, and from the ancient songs with which they observed it.

The most singular and serious authors who painted the histories of this land and composed songs, who were Nezahualcoyotzin, the king of Texcoco, and the two princes of Mexico, Xiuhcozcatzin and Tzahuatzin, say and declare by them that the world had and has four ages; the first was from its origin, which they called Atonatio, meaning sun of water, because this age was ended and consumed with the flood; the second they called Tlalchitonatiuc, meaning sun of earth, which ended with a great earthquake, in which the earth opened up in many places, and pieces of rocks and mountains fell and rolled in such a way that almost all the men perished, in whose age were the giants whom they called Ouinametitzucuil.

The third they called Hecactonactiuh, which is the same as sun of air, because the wind it made then was so great and so fierce that it tore down all the buildings and trees and even crumbled the rocks and many of the dwellers died, and because those who escaped from this calamity found a large quantity of monkeys in the places and towns, they said they had changed into this species of animals, giving rise to the much mentioned fable of the monkeys. Those who possessed this new world in this age were the Olmecs and Xicalancas, and according to what it seems by their histories, they came in ships or boats along the eastern part to the land of Papuha, from where they started to settle it, and in the lands that are at the banks of the Athoiac River, which is the one that runs between the city of Los Angeles and the city of Tula, they found some of the giants who had escaped from the second age, who, being robust people confident in their strength and largeness of body, ruled over the new settlers, in such a way that they had them so oppressed as if they were their slaves, for which reason the caudillos and principal people of the Olmecs and Xicalancas sought ways to be able to free themselves from this servitude, and so it was that in the very solemn feast that they made for them, after they were full and satisfied and drunk, with their own weapons they finished them off and consumed them, by which deed they ended up free and exempt from this plague, and their dominion and command increased. And being in the greatest prosperity, a man came to this land whom they called Quetzalcoatl and by another name, Huemac, a virgin, just and holy, he who came from the eastern part and taught the natural law and established the fast, avoiding all vices and sins; the first who placed and established a cross, whom they called God of the rains and of health; who, seeing the little fruit that he was making in the teaching of these peoples, returned by the way from where he had come, and at the time that he went away, he had told the natives of those times that he would come in the coming times, in a year that would be called ce acatl, and that by then his doctrine would be received and his children would be lords, they would possess the earth, and many other things that afterwards they saw very clearly; who, once he had gone away from there, a few days later the terrible destruction mentioned of the third age occurred, and then that very memorable building of the city of Chulula, which was like another second tower of Babel that these people were building, was destroyed, and afterwards they built a temple (those-who escaped in the ruins of them) to Quetzalcoatl, whom they placed as God of the air, and according to the histories mentioned and the annals, it appears that this happened some years after the incarnation of Christ, our

Lord, and from this time here the fourth age entered in, which they said was called Tletonatiuh, because it is to end with fire (Ibid., I:529-530).

CHAPTER I.

Dealing with the creation of the world, and its four ages that the historians of this New Spain gave, and the end of each one of them.

Of the most serious authors and historians that existed in the antiquity of these natives, Quetzalcoatl is found to have been the first; and of the modern ones, Nezahualcoyotzin king of Texcoco, and the two princes of Mexico, Itzcoatzin and Xiuhcozcatzin, the sons of King Huitzilihuitzin, without [considering] many others that there were (which I will mention wherever it may be necessary). They declare by their histories that the god Teotloquenahuaque, Tlachiquale, Ipalnemoani, Ilhuicahica, Tlalticpaque, which means according to the true meaning the universal God of all things, Creator of them, and by whose will all creatures live, Lord of the heaven and of the earth, etc., who, after having created all visible and invisible things, created the first parents of men, from where all the rest proceeded; and the dwelling and habitation that he gave them was the world which they say has four ages. The first, which was from its origin, called by them Atonatiuh, which means sun of water; which means, in an allegorical sense, that first age of the world that ended with the Flood and inundation of the waters, with which all men were drowned and all things created perished.

They called the second age Tlalchitonatiuh, which means sun of earth, because it ended with earthquakes, the land opening up in many parts, and being submerged, and with mountains and rocks being torn down, in such a way that nearly all men perished, in which age and time the giants lived that they called quinametintzocuilhicxime.

They called the third age Ecatonatiuh, which means sun of air, because this age died with air; in which the wind that

41

occurred then was so much and so strong that it tore down all the buildings and trees and even broke the rocks apart, and most of the men perished: and because those who escaped this calamity found a large number of monkeys that the wind must have brought from other parts, they said that the men had become this species of animals, giving birth to this fable so talked about of the monkeys.

Those who possessed this New World in this third age were the Olmecs and Xicalancas; and according to what is found in their histories, they came in ships or boats from the part of the East to the land of Potonchan, from where they started to populate it; and on the banks of the Atoyac River, which is the one that goes between the city of Los Angeles and Cholula, they found some of the giants who had escaped from the calamity and destruction of the second age; who, being robust people and confident in their strength and their large bodies, they dominated the new inhabitants in such a way that they had them as oppressed as if they were their slaves; for this reason the captains and principal people looked for ways to be able to free themselves from this servitude, and it was at a very solemn feast that they made for them: after they were completely full and drunk, with their own weapons they finished them off and consumed them, with which deed they ended up free and exempt from that subjugation, and their own dominion and command increased.

And being in the greatest prosperity of it, a man arrived at this land whom they called Quetzalcoatl and whom some called Huemac because of his great virtues, considering him as just, holy, and good; teaching them by works and words the road of virtue and saving them from vices and sins, giving laws and good doctrine; and to restrain them from their pleasures and dishonesties he instituted the fast among them, and the first one who worshiped and placed the cross that they called Quiahuiteotlchicahualizteotl and others called Tonacaquahuitl, which means: god of the rains and of health and tree of sustenance or of life. Who having preached the things mentioned in all the greatest of the cities of the Olmecs and Xicalancas, and especially in the city of Cholula, where he most attended, and seeing the small amount of fruit that he was making with his doctrine, he returned by the same place from where he had come, which was by that of the East, disappearing along the coast of Coatzacoalco; and at the time that he was bidding farewell to these people he told them that in the coming times, in a year that would be called Ce Acatl, he would return, and then his doctrine would be received and their children would be lords and would possess the land, and that they and their descendants would go through many calamities and persecutions; and many other prophecies that afterwards were seen very clearly.

Quetzalcoatl, by literal interpretation, means serpent of precious feathers; by allegorical meaning, very wise man; and Huemac, some say that they gave him this name because he imprinted and stamped his hands upon a rock, as if it were in soft wax, as a testimony that everything that he had said would be fulfilled. Others want to say that it means the man with the large or powerful hand. Who, after he left, a few days later the destruction and devastation mentioned of the third age of the world occurred; and then the destruction occurred of that building and of such a memorable and sumptuous tower of the city of Cholula, which was like another second tower of Babel, which these people built with almost the same designs, with people built with almost the same designs, with the wind breaking it up. And afterwards, those who escaped the destruction of the third age, in the ruins of it, built a temple to Quetzalcoatl, whom they placed as god of the air, because of the air having been the cause of their destruction, they understanding that this calamity was sent from his hand; and they also called him Ce Acatl, which was the name of the year of his coming. And it appears by the histories mentioned and by the annals, that the above-mentioned occurred a few years after the Incarnation of Christ our Lord; and since this time, the fourth age entered here, which they said was called

Tletonatiuh, which means sun of fire, because they said that this fourth age of the world is to end by fire. Quetzalcoatl was a good-looking man, with a serious appearance, white, and bearded. His clothing was a long tunic (Ibid., II:7-9).

HISTORY OF THE TOLTEC LORDS

Account of the creation of the world and of what concerns the creation of the world and origin of the Indians. Only God knows all things; but whatever it has been possible to learn, according to the Toltecs, is what follows.

The Toltecs understood and learned about the creation of the world, and how the Tloque Nahuaque created it and the other things that are in it, such as plants, mountains, birds, water, and fishes; they also learned how God created man and a woman, from where men descended and multiplied, and on this they add many fables that, for the sake of brevity, are not put here, and it should not come as a shock that the same thing has been done by the other nations of the world; and they say that the world was created in the year of ce tecpatl, and this time until the flood they called Atonatiuh, which means, age of sun of water, because the world was destroyed by the flood. And in the histories of the Toltecs it is found that this age and first world, as they called it, lasted one thousand seven hundred sixteen years, that men were destroyed with very great downpours and lightning bolts from the heaven and all the earth without anything remaining, and the highest mountains caxtol moletltli hid themselves inside the waters, which are fifteen cubits; and from here, they also add other fables, and how the men went back to multiplying from the few who escaped from this destruction inside a toptlipetlacali, that this word almost means, closed ark; and how afterwards, with the men multiplying, they made a very high, and strong, zacuali, which means, the extremely high tower, to shelter themselves in it when the second world was again destroyed. At the best time the languages were changed, and not understanding each other, they went to various parts of the world, and the Toltecs, who were as many as seven companions with their wives, who understood the language of each other, came to these parts, first having passed great lands and seas, living in the caves and going through great work until coming to this land, which they found to be good and fertile for their habitation; and they say that they wandered one hundred four years through different parts of the world until arriving in Huehue Tlapalan, their fatherland, which was in ce tecpatl, that from the time the flood had occurred it had been five hundred twenty years, which are five ages, and after one thousand seven hundred fifteen years had gone by since the flood, they were destroyed in a very great hurricane that carried away the trees, the rocks, houses and people and great buildings, although many men and women escaped, mainly those who were able to escape in caves and places where this great hurricane couldn't reach them; and after several days or the time had gone by, they came out of the caves to see how the land had ended up, and they found it all covered and populated by monkeys, and they were in darkness all this time without seeing the sun or the moon, which the air had brought them: and from this the Indians invented a fable, in which they say that men turned into monkeys. They called this age or second world, according to them they call it, Ecactonatiuh, which means sun of air, and after they escaped, they went to rebuilding again and to multiplying, and in the year of tochtli, which had been one thousand three hundred forty-seven years since the second calamity, and 4779 since the creation of the world, and there they have in their history that the sun stood still for one natural day without being moved from one place, and they add a fable, saying that as the mosquito saw the sun so suspended and pensive, he told him, "Lord of the world, why are you so suspended and pensive and don't do your job as you are ordered to do? What, do you want to destroy the world as you usually do?" And many other fabulous words, and the mosquito, seeing that he was quiet and wasn't answering him, went and bit him on one

leg, and finding himself bit, he started to travel along his
course again as always. One hundred fifty-eight years after the
great hurricane, and four thousand nine hundred ninety-four
years after the creation of the world, there was another
destruction experienced by those of this land who were the
Quinametin giants who lived in this corner, which is now
called New Spain, which destruction was from a great earthquake, which swallowed them up and killed them, with the
high volcanic mountains erupting, such that all were destroyed
without anyone escaping, and if any escaped, it was from
among those who were more toward the interior land; and also
many of the Toltecs died as did the Chichimecs their adjacent
neighbors, which was in the year of ce tecpatl; and this age
they called Tlacchitonatiuh, which means sun of earth. In the
year of 5097 of the creation of the world, which was ce tecpatl,
and one hundred four years after the total destruction of the
Quinametin giants, having quiet peace in all this new world, all
the wise Toltecs, astrologers as well as the other arts, gathered
together in Huehue Tlapalan, the leading city of their dominion, where they discussed many things, such as events, calamities that they experienced and movements of the heavens since
the creation of the world, as well as many other things, which,
because of having burned their histories, it hasn't been possible to learn or reach beyond what has been written here,
among which they added the leap year to adjust the solar year
with the equinox and many other curiosities, as will be seen in
the tables and patterns of them, of their years, months, weeks
and days, signs and plants as they understood them, and many
other curiosities. It had been one hundred sixty-six years since
they adjusted their years and times with the equinox, and two
hundred seventy years since the giants had been destroyed,
when the sun and the moon eclipsed and the earth trembled
and the rocks were broken up and many other things and signs
happened, although there was no calamity in the men, which
was in the year of ce calli, which, when this count is adjusted
with ours, comes to be at the same time when Christ our Lord

suffered, and they say that it was in the first days of the year. The Toltecs came to understand these and many and many other things from the creation of the world, and almost until in our times, which, as I have said, for the sake of brevity are not put in according to how they appear in their histories and paintings, mainly of the original, I mean of the things that are found of painting and history, but everything is very brief compared to the histories that the first archbishop of Mexico ordered burned.

It had been three hundred years since the sun and the moon eclipsed, and four hundred thirty-eight since the destruction of the Quinametin giants, and 5486 since the creation of the world, when Chalcatzin and Tlacamihtzin, gentlemen and very principal descendants of the royal household of the Toltecs, started to want to raise themselves up with the kingdom, wanting to take it from the legitimate successor, after having been in quiet peace for many years, which was in the year of Acatl. They were exiled and had some wars, until they were cast out of the city Tlachicatzin in the region of Huey Tlapalan, their homeland, with all their allies and families, men as well as women, there was a plentiful number of them, they went out in the following year of ce tecpatl exiled from all that land, as will be seen in what follows, and by our count, 439 years after the incarnation of Christ our Lord (Ibid., I:263-265).

SIGNS AND WONDERS BEFORE THE COMING OF CORTES (CHICHIMEC HISTORY, CHAPTER LXXII)

In the year 1510, which they called macuili toxtli, was when a great light appeared on many nights that originated from the eastern part, rose high, and seemed to be in a pyramid shape, and with some flames of fire, which caused such great admiration and fear in all the land, that even those who were very learned in astrology and knowledge of their divinations and prophecies were confounded; although they had information from very far back, and they found in their histories that the times were already approaching in which the things were to be

fulfilled which Quetzalcoatl and the other philosophers and
wise ancient ones had foretold; and those to whom most care
was given were the kings Nezahualpiltzintli and Motecuhzoma,
as persons in whom the rigor of the changes of the empire were
to be carried out; and as the king of Tetzcuco was so consumed
in all the sciences that they achieved and knew, especially the
astrology confirmed with the prophecies of their forebears, in
addition to the affliction in which it was seen, he scorned his
kingdom and dominion; and so in this season he ordered the
captains and caudillos of his armies to cease the continual wars
that they were having with the Tlaxcaltecs, Huexotzincas, and
Atlixcas, for the military exercise and sacrifice of their false
gods; and against the remote provinces where they had their
borders and garrisons, and to just guard them and defend them
without making any entrances, so that they would enjoy with all
peace and tranquility the little bit of time that was left to him of
dominion and command. On the other part, King
Motecuhzoma had a very great desire to communicate with him
about the signs, and of his operations; and as they were incom-
patible and conflicting, King Nezahual-piltzintli, because of the
great grief that he had from the death and treachery that
Motecuhzoma had done against his son-in-law, Prince
Macuilmalinatzin, and this because he was also forming other
complaints, one of which was the justice that was so severe and
public that Nezahualpiltzintli had done against his sister,
Queen Chachiuhnenetzin, and the other complaints also of two
other punishments that he had done, the one against Prince
Huexotzincatzin his nephew, and the other against his father-
in-law, the lord of Azcaputzalco Tezozomoc, the two kings got
together and each one being satisfied of his complaint, they
talked at great length about what the heaven was threatening
against them, and the king of Tetzcuco said that everything
would be fulfilled without there being anything they could do
about it; and for King Motecuhzoma to take note of what he
considered his kingdom and dominion to be, he proposed to
him that he would play him in a barter that if he won three

stripes in a ball game against him, he would give him three mountain roosters, and that of them he only wanted the spurs, so that he would realize how much he valued everything that he had and possessed; and so the two kings played ball, and with Motecuhzoma having won two continuous stripes, so that now he only had one left to win in order to become lord of the Alculhuas, he started to get happy and rejoice very much; and the king of Tetzcuco, who had purposely made himself the loser, told King Motecuhzoma that very quickly that pleasure of imagining himself being made the absolute lord of the whole empire would end, and he would realize how changeable and perishable it was to command and enjoy the things that the world offers, and that in testimony that what he was saying was certain and true, it would become obvious in the course of the game, because although he had won two stripes, he wouldn't win the game against him; and proceeding in that way in the game, although King Motecuhzoma did everything possible to win the stripe that he was lacking, he was unable to: Nezahualpiltzintli won by getting all three stripes; and having celebrated them, and having dealt with other items of business, the king of Tetzcuco went back to his house and court.

Each day new signs and great wonders and portents were seen, which announced the ruin and total destruction of all this land and change in the entire empire (Ibid., II:81, 182).

Don Mariano Fernandez de Echevarria y Veytia (1720-1778)

Don Mariano Fernandez de Echevarria y Veytia (Mariano Veytia) was born in Puebla de los Angeles, Mexico, 16 July 1720, (died 1778) a descendant of Spanish royalty, a friend and associate of King Carlos III of Spain. He lived and wrote much while in Europe, serving as attorney for the Spanish Royal Councils and ultimately becoming Trustee Attorney General.

This excerpt is a portion of his two volume work titled Historia Antigua de Mexico. It is taken from the first English translation, Ancient America Rediscovered.

CHAPTER XIV

Of the great eclipse and earthquake that the Indians mention as having observed in these regions, which seems to have been that of the death of Jesus Christ.

These natives indicate another singular event in their histories with great exactness, which later served them as a fixed era for their chronological calculations. They say that 166 years after the correction of their calendar, at the beginning of the year that was indicated with the hieroglyph of the House in the number ten, being a full moon, the sun was eclipsed at midday, the solar body being totally covered, such that the earth became darkened so much that the stars appeared and it seemed like night, and at the same time an earthquake was felt as horrible as they had ever experienced, because the stones crashing against one another were broken into pieces, and the earth opened up in many parts. Confused and bewildered, they believed that the end of the third age of the world had already arrived, which, according to the predictions of their wise men in Huehuetlapallan, should end in strong earthquakes, in whose violence many living people would perish, and mankind would suffer the third calamity; but the earthquake ceasing entirely and the sun once again being uncovered perfectly, everyone was found to be whole, without any living persons having perished, and this caused them such great wonder that they noted it in their histories with singular care. Following these calculations, and adjusted to the comparison of the tables, this event should be placed in the year 4066 of the world, which was indicated with this character as can be seen in the tables, and precisely 166 years after the adjustment of the calendar; and because of the circumstances surrounding this eclipse and earthquake, it was impossible for it to be any other than that which was observed at the death of Jesus Christ Our Lord, having suffered it in the thirty-third year of his age, and so it seems that the incarnation of the Word should be placed in the year 4034 of the world, which the Indians indicated with the same hieroglyph of the House in the number 4, and I have noted it that way in the tables, and with this calculation following the chronological order that they observed, counting the years from one memorable event to another with the assignment of the hieroglyph of the year in which they fell, I have been able to coordinate it perfectly with our years in the year 1519, in which Cortez landed at Veracruz, as will be seen in the discourse of this history.

By this it should not be understood that I take it upon myself to decide on such a questionable point, in which so many great minds have set their pens in such a learned and knowledgeable manner, giving accuracy preference to the Indians over the great number of illustrious talents who have dealt with this subject with great diligence and study in this matter; although it isn't strange for God to have revealed to these small ones what he hid from the wise, as he did with the invention of the leap days; but I do say that among the multitudes of opinions, on the age of the world when the Word became incarnate, there is a variation from three thousand and so many years to five thousand and so many, which is almost two thousand years of difference, and this calculation of the Indians is a perfect average between these two extremes. The chronicle of Auberte [the book has "Hauberto"], Father Suarez (1) and the authors he quotes vary by just a few years from the calculations of the Indians; and finally, having to follow the calculation of the Indians according to the historian laws, and their chronological method in assigning their years in which the events occurred, and comparing them to our corresponding years, in order not to fall into the anachronisms that the authors of some of the documents that I have fallen into, because of trying to do the count from memory, I assumed the material work of perfecting the tables, and on them I have followed my calculations, precisely observing the hieroglyphs and numbers that the Indians assigned, as will be seen in the discourse of the history by the references that I will be doing for the satisfaction of the curious.

The Gentlemen Boturini, in his mentioned work, says that the first Christian Indians who then perfectly understood their chronology and studied ours with all curiosity left us the knowledge as from the creation of the world until the mentioned birth of Christ, 5199 years had passed, which is the same opinion or calculation of the seventy. Among the monuments that he gathered, I have not been able to find the one that enlightened him with this information, because they wrote most of them without chronology, that is, following the method of the historical charts, referring to the events, assigning only the symbol or hieroglyph of the year in which they occurred, for example, the Flood in the year of one flint, the suspension of the sun in the year of eight Rabbits, the great earthquake in the year of ten Houses, etc.; but they do not enter into finding out what year of the creation or of the Christian era they correspond to, and the most precise just say the centuries or the years that had passed from one event to another, regularly leaving out the broken years(2). The one who put the most care into the chronology was Fernando de Alba, [Ixtlilxochitl] seeking to compare their eras and reduce their years to ours; but in four manuscripts that I have of his, he varies considerably with a difference of hundreds of years from one calculation to another, and in each one of his narration obvious anachronisms are found at each step. The cause was his having done the counts and calculations from memory (3) and without forming tables; so asserts Boturini himself in his books, and he told me repeatedly that to write the history that he was pondering and that we have in our hands it was necessary to be bound to the tables and work on them, adapting the events with special care to the hieroglyphs of the years; because in assigning these hieroglyphs the Indians were very precise, but not in the number of them that they would assign from one event to another, especially when they were counting by ages or centuries, because then they would regularly omit the extra broken years; and I have experienced it as he was telling about it; therefore, above all, I sought to finish the tables that Boturini himself started in his own hand, and tied to them precisely I have indicated the eras, in which he didn't make the world more than 4033 years old when Jesus Christ was born, and what is more worthy of reflection, Boturini himself, in the mentioned tables that he formed in his own hand, indicates the year in this way: three Tecpatl, 4033 Nativitatis Domini, from which it appears that he got the same count, and therefore, from the following year, which is the year 4034, he starts to indicate the years of the Christian era in the same way that I do, and it is expressed in the tables; and in the year 4056 he puts this sign in the margin: oIHS, which means Crucifixion of Jesus. in which time the earthquake occurred, and so I am persuaded that he was mistaken in this assertion from his book, because, as I have already said in other places, and he confesses, he wrote from memory and without having access to the documents that he gathered.

FOOTNOTES ON CHAPTER XIV (KINGSBOROUGH)

1. Suarez In. 3, Part. D. Thomae, vo1ume I, quaest. 1, art. 6, Disp. 6, sect. 1.

2. By the expression "quebrados" [broken] are meant the odd years over and above a Mexican age or century.

3. Echeverria's assertion that Don Ferdinand de Alba Ixtlilxochitl and Boturini had both been guilty of anachronisms, from placing too much dependence on their memory in framing their chronological computations, should be understood of each of them in a different sense. He evidently means that the former writer had fallen into error, from not having formed tables such as he had himself made use of, the better to adjust the signs employed in the Mexican calendar to our years; and that the latter, when in Spain, could not have been able to consult the paintings which he had left behind him in Mexico (Veytia, 148-151).

CHAPTER XV

Of the coming to these lands of a wonderful man to whom they gave the names of Quetzalcohuatl, Cocolcan, and Hueman.

Several years after the great eclipse, in a year that was indicated with the hieroglyph of the Reed in the number one (which according to the tables seems to have been the year 63 of Jesus Christ), a white and bearded man of good stature came to these regions through the northern part, dressed in an ankle-length tunic adorned with red crosses, barefoot, his head uncovered, and a staff in his hand, whom some call Quetzalcohuatl, others Cocolcan, and others Hueman.

They say that he was just and holy, that he taught them a good law, counseling them to overcome their own passions and appetites, to hate vice, and to love virtue; he instituted the forty-day fast, mortification and penitence with shedding of blood, he acquainted them with the cross, promising them, by means of that sign, serenity in the air, the necessary rain, the preservation of their populations, bodily health, and the relief of all their needs. He told them about a triune and one God, (1) taking the opportunity to explain to them this mystery of rocks and triangular poles and other similar figures, of the Virgin birth, and other mysteries that they later mixed with fables and mistakes, as will be seen later on; and crossing the land of Anahuac and the settlements of the Olmecs, he stayed for a time in the city of Chollolan.

Although they do not say the exact number of years that had gone by after the great eclipse until the appearance of this venerable man, they indicate the hieroglyph of the year, which was the Reed in the number 1, and in the suppositions of its having been the eclipse that occurred at the death of Jesus Christ, which we have placed in the year 33 from the incarnation, the first one after it that is indicated with the Reed in the number 1 is that of 63 A.D., 30 years after the eclipse, as can be seen in the tables.

Among all the authors who have written of things of the Indies, there is none who does not talk about this wonderful man, but all with confusion according to the knowledge that they acquired, whether mixed with fables, whether explained with allegories given either by common people or by well-educated people misunderstood by the writers, such that they make him a God, King, Priest, Magician, and finally, in these narrations there are a thousand oddities and contradictions that cause notable revulsion. Therefore, it seems to me that I must declare not only what I find in the authentic monuments, manuscripts, and histories that I have gathered, but also the rule that I follow about this famous man and the foundations that persuade me, although it may seem a digression from the main topics, for not only is it one of the most curious points, but also one of the most necessary points to understand the origin of many of the rites and ceremonies that the Spanish found established among these nations at the time of the conquest, and it is no less important to correct the multitude of errors that most of our writers make in the foundations of some of the cities, and the coming and establishment of several nations.

Father Torquemada, (2) who gathered much ancient information and brought it to light in his Monarquia Indiana [Indian Monarchy] in the same way that it was given by the persons from whom he was informed, without stopping to criticize the difficulties and contradictions that conflict with each other, talks several times in his work of Quetzalcohautl, and says that he was a king of Tollan, a priest, a necromancer, a magician, a liar, superstitious, [see page 21] human and merciful, very honest, very chaste, a pursuer of evil doers, a sufferer of insults, a wise astrologer, a skilled craftsman in works of gold and silver, a very expert farmer who taught them the cultivation of many plants~ and finally, adorned with so many good and evil qualities contrary one to another that they do not fit in one individual. And the best part is, that neither his magic nor his wisdom were sufficient to keep him from being deceived and overcome by the sorcerer Titlacuahua, who first persuaded him to take a trip to the kingdom of Tlapallan, and afterwards tried to obstruct his way, without the reason for one or the other being known. Finally the life of this man and his character, according to this author in the different places in which he speaks of him, is a combination of passages that do not fit in one individual, especially if we add the one that also asserts that the remembrance of this man remained so permanent and so venerable that they not only observed the moralities that he taught them and the rites and customs that he introduced keeping his prophecies very much in mind, the fulfillment of which they were expecting, but also that those who came to reign in Mexico did not receive the kingdom as lords themselves, but as lieutenants of Quetzalcohuatl, it being certain and constant in all the histories of the Indians that he was not king of Tollan, nor was Tollan founded until many years later, and Mexico a great many years more, nor were his four disciples the first founders of the lordship of Tlaxcala, but other very different ones, as will be seen later. And even though some of these passages this author confesses are fables, others he gives as certain and established, equating them with events of sacred and profane history.

Antonio de Herrera says that (3) Quetzalcohuatl, which means god of the air, is made to be the founder of Chollolan, (4) that he came from toward the north by sea and landed at Panuco with a company of new people who penetrated to Tollan, where they were well received, and not being able to subsist there because of Mexico already being founded and all the land settled, they went on to Chollolan, where they settled and later spread to Huaxaca and Misteca. That the word Quetzalcohuatl, literally translated means God of the air, there will be no one who is moderately educated in the Mexican language who will say so; but as in later times the Chollotecs worshiped Quetzalcohuatl as the God of the air, that is where Herrera, or those who communicated this information to him, want his name to mean that, and confusing the coming of the Olmecs with that of the Toltecs, and Huemac (another ancient wise person who came with the Toltecs) withQuetzalcohautl, he postpones the founding of Chollolan to that of Tollan and Mexico, and it seems that he gives Quetzalcohautl and his associates the name of Toltecatl, which means craftsman, because in Tollan they started to teach, although he calls Tollan Tula, and instead of saying Toltecatl he says Tulotec.

Quetzalcohautl was neither king nor chief of any nation he came to inhabit, nor a magician, nor a necromancer, sorcerer, or liar, [see page 21] but a venerable, just, and holy man, who with works and words taught the road of truth through the overcoming of ones passions, mortification, fast and penitence. In the worship of just one God he enlightened these natives of the Sublime Mystery of the August Trinity, the coming of the son of God to the World, the Virgin birth, the passion of the Lord and his death on the holy wood of the cross, whose powerful sign he manifested to them, and he was worshiped by them, inspiring a great hope in them of achieving the universal remedy, through him, of all their needs. He made them various prophecies, of which the one of the destruction of the tower of Chollolan, and that of the coming of some white bearded peoples from the east who would take possession of the land, (5) were very notable, and both the one and the other were fulfilled purposely in all their circumstances, as we shall see. For the person who did all this to have been a magician, necromancer or sorcerer, a minister of the devil, is something so repulsive that in itself it becomes unbelievable, and on the contrary, according to the time in which the Indian historians indicate his coming, it seems consistent that it was some apostle or disciple of Jesus Christ, who, after his passion and death, traveled to these parts to spread in them the preaching of the gospel to verify the prophecy of David: Their line is gone out through all the earth, and their words to the end of the world (6) and fulfill the precept of Christ to his apostles: Go ye into all the world, and preach the gospel to every creature. (7) Because one who says "All the World" is not excluding America, which is half of the world's globe, and one who says "every creature" is not excluding the inhabitants of America, who then were a very considerable portion of creatures; and that this precept of Christ to the apostles is to be understood in the generality that it sounds like of the world and creatures is the opinion of St. Gregory, St. Thomas, St. Juan Crisostomo, (8) Teophilato, Eutimio, (9) the cardinals Hugo and Cayetano, (10) and many other exponents, some of whom assert that in the space of forty years following the death of Christ the apostles preached throughout the world. With the Indians indicating the coming of Quetzalcohuatl thirty years afterwards, it agrees well with this opinion, and all the doctrine that he taught being in agreement with the new gospel law, we must believe that it was one of the holy apostles, and that not as a natural but rather as a miraculous act he walked throughout this new world, and he preached throughout, leaving many traces and signs that survive to our times, as we are going to see.

FOOTNOTES ON CHAPTER XV (KINGSBOROUGH)

1. Reserving for another place proofs from Clavijero's History of California, of the Indians of that peninsula believing in a Trinity, and in an incarnation of the Son of God, we shall here only observe that the doctrine of a Trinity was known in many parts of America: for example, in Mexico, Yucatan, and Peru; in Nicaragua; amongst the Muyscas, a civilized people of New Granada; in Paraguay, and according to some accounts, even in Chile and amongst the Indians dwelling on the banks of the Orinoco. Statements of this curious fact are to be found in the second chapter of the fourth book of the third part of Oviedo's unpublished General History of the Indies; in the second part of the inedited Noticias Historiales of Pedro Simon; in Acosta's Natural and Moral History of the Indies; in Renessad's Chronicle of Chiapa; in Cogolludo's History of Yucatan; in Torquemada's Indian Monarchy; in the first book of the third volume of the Saggio di Storia Americana by the Abbe Gilii; in Calancha' s Chronicle of the Order of Saint Augustin in Peru; and in Garcia's Predicacion del Evangelio en el Nuevo Mundo. Echevarria's [Veytia] statement that the Mexicans adored a Trinity in Unity receives great confirmation from the following passage of the first part of an inedited Treatise of Torribio de Benavente, which is preserved in manuscript in the library of the Escorial, who affirms that the people of Tlaxcala, Huexocinco and Chollola (three states contiguous to Mexico) worshiped one God under three names: "Without the said festivals, there were many others in each province, and they served each demon in their own way with sacrifices and fasts and other diabolical offerings, especially in Tlaxcala, Huexocinco, Chollola, which were lordships in themselves. In all these provinces, which are

near each other and came from the same ancestry, they all worshiped and had their God as the main one to whom they gave three names. `Ancient rites, sacrifices, and idolatries of the Indians of New Spain and of their conversion to the Faith.' Diego Duran, another ancient Spanish author, whose History of Mexico was given by Juan de Tobar to Acosta, (although the latter nowhere acknowledges the obligation which he was under to a writer, from whom he appears to have borrowed almost all that he wrote concerning the ancient history of the Mexicans,) confirms in the following passage of that history the previous testimony of Benavente: "It is noteworthy that the present figure was solemnized in the name of the Father, which Tota means, in order that we know that they reverenced the Father and the Son and the Holy Ghost, and said Tota, Teopiltzin, and Yolometl, the words mean our father and our son, and the heart of both, making a festival to each one in particular and to all three in one, where the knowledge is noted that there was a Trinity among these people (Veytia, 152-156).

2. Torquemada, Monarquia Ind. Page 3, book 3, chapter 7. Id. Lib. 4, chapter 14.

3. Herrera dec. 2, book 7, chapter 2. Id. Dec. 5, book 2, chapter 11. [Herrera dec. 2, book 7,chapter 2, folio 219.]

4. Id. Dec. 3, book 2, chapter 11, folio 79.

5. The prophecies here ascribed to Quetzalcohuatl must remind us of Christ's famous predictions respecting the destruction of the temple at Jerusalem and the conquest of Judea by the Romans.

6. Psalms 19:4.

7. Mark 16:15.

8. Crisostomo Hom. 76. Sup. Mat.

9. Teoph et Eutrum. In Math. 24.

10. Hugo et Caiet. In Math. 28, et Marc. 16.

CHAPTER XVI.

The vestiges found in New Spain of Quetzalcohuatl denote his having been one of the holy Apostles.

The sovereign sign of the cross, a figure of the crucified, a scandal to the Jews and foolishness to the gentiles according to the Apostle (l), is the insignia and very character of the Christian disciple of Christ and professor of the gospel law, and this was what Quetzalcohuatl manifested and let these natives know, forming crosses in different manners, which he exhibited and placed in many parts for it to be venerated, and this knowledge was found by the Spanish when they arrived in these parts, so constant throughout this new world because of the tradition from fathers to sons, as testified by all our writers. Herrera says (2) that when Grijalva discovered the New Spain, he gave it this name because of the many lime houses and the singing, towers, and crosses that they found in those settlements that they saw. Cortez found a large cross on a beautiful stone wall that was worshiped from very ancient times in Acazamil or Cozumel; and Gomara (3) asserts that this place was considered a common shrine of all the surrounding islands and that there was no town that did not have its shrine of stone or of another material. Crosses were also found in Chollolan, in Tollan, in Texcoco, and in other parts, and generally the sign of the cross was considered the God of the rain among all these natives, because this being such a necessary asset for the success of their planting, Quetzalcohuatl taught them the impetration of god through the cross; and it arose from here that in later times, with those first lights obscured or extinguished, they worshiped it as God of the rain and of the air that conducts it. Finally, they are all in agreement that this man wore a white, ankle length tunic adorned with red crosses, and anyone who took care to extol this sovereign sign and to mark himself with it gives more signs of being a Christian than a gentile, of an apostle than a necromancer, of a saint than of a magician and deceiver.

I am not unaware of the fact that Father Torquemada (4) wants to persuade that the crosses that Francisco de Montejo found when he started the conquest of Yucatan, especially in the province of Totolxiuh, and the one that Cortez found in Acuzamil, were placed there a little before the Spanish arrived there, by a gentile priest named Chilacambal whom they consider as a great prophet, and that this was the one who predicted to them that within a brief time some white, bearded people would go there from the east, who would wear that insignia which their gods couldn't attain, and that this people would rule the land.

But about the inconsistencies and contradictions that this persuasion includes, which Father Gregorio Garcia (5) puts forth in the book that he printed with the title of Predicacion del Evangelio en el Nuevo Mundo [Preaching the Gospel in the New World], he adds that it is necessary to prove that this same professor walked all of New Spain and Peru, planting crosses and making the same prophesy, for one and another were found in agreement throughout America, as is seen in all our historians of both kingdoms. But inasmuch as my concern is only New Spain, I will not go out of it to show the vestiges that this venerable man left of the gospel truth.

Father Torquemada (6) himself talks about the miraculous cross of the place of Quautolco that they commonly call Guatulco; and although he says that this was put in this place by Father Martin de Valencia or another of his companions in those early times, this is mere arbitrary conjecture, which Father Garcia refuted with solid reasons in the mentioned place (7); and Father Joachim Brulio, in the History of Peru of his religious order of St. Augustine(8), asserts that this holy cross was venerated in that place since very ancient times. That is confirmed by Father Gregorio Garcia, who adds the miracle that occurred when the heretic Francisco Drake, who landed there, tried to burn it and was unable to do so; for it was thrown into a fire three times and the fire did it no harm; and even though he covered it with fish and tar to get it to burn, he was unsuccessful. This holy cross is venerated at the present time in the city of Guaxacac, to where it was moved by Bishop Juan de Cervantes, and at the Convent of Discalzed Carmelites of Puebla de los Angeles they venerate a cross made of an arm of this one, which was taken there and placed in a chapel of the presbytery by Mr. Antonio de Cervantes Carvajal, a canon of that church and nephew of the mentioned bishop.

Mr. Bartolome de las Casas, the Bishop of Chiapas, after a serious report was made on the case, asserts in an apology of his, which manuscript is kept in the Convent of Santo Domingo in Mexico, that it is known because of a very ancient tradition of those natives that that cross was brought by a white, bearded man, dressed to the knuckles in a white, ankle-length tunic, that he brought other disciples with him, and that these disciples told their grandparents about the mysteries of the Trinity and the Virgin birth, and they taught them the fast and penitence. These are the same signs that the Indian historians of QuetzaIcohuatl give.

And to convince that the worship that they gave to this holy cross was as ancient as the place, and not from the times immediately prior to the conquest, as Father Torquemada suggests, I am going to give irrefutable proof in the very name of the place, for as all [place names] are significant in the Mexican language, many times I have taken advantage of them to resolve my questions, and always with good effects. The true name of this place is Quauhtolco; that is how it is written by the Indian authors and those who know and perfectly possess the Nahuatl language, not Quanhtochco, as fathers Torquemada and Garcia write; the latter is a very different place close to Orizaba and the town of Cordoba, which the Spanish corrupted because they couldn't pronounce it, calling it Guatusco, and they call Quauhtolco Guatulco. Now this name Quauhtolco is a compound of Quautli, which means the wood, from the verb toloa, which means to venerate by bowing the head, and the particle co, which denotes place, and thus Quauhtolco means place where one worships or bows to the pole. And so the worship of the cross was as ancient as its name was in this place, and maybe even more ancient, since it took its name from it.

Father Garcia (9) makes mention of another prodigious cross that was found in the sierra of Meztitlan, and he quotes Esteban de Salazar, a Carthusian monk, who was previously an Augustian monk, as Father Calancha (10) says, whose words he mentioned that are copied from the work of Father Garcia, and afterwards I compared them with the book of Father Salazar entitled Discurso sabre el Credo [Discourse on the Creed], which is the one that Boturini mentions in his catalog of documents that he gathered, and they are these: "On a point of a very high sierra in a very distinguished place, which took its name from the antiquity and sculpture that it has on that peak cut from the mountain, as did all the heavily populated and very wide mountains that they call Meztitlan; because Meztli, in the Nahuatl or Mexican language, means moon, and tetl, stone, crag or cliff, and titlan, on the cliff, so that Meztitlan means the moon over the cliff. On that rocky cliff, at that very high and almost inaccessible place, a cross is cut in relief at the right hand of the river in tau fashion, which is a T, worked in squares like a chessboard, one square of the color of the stone, which is very white, and another of a very perfect blue, one cubit high (as judged by sight from a great distance away), and in front of it a half moon of the same size, on the left hand of the cliff, also carved in relief on it and worked with the same squares and colors. Among that people there are none who have any knowledge about when, or in what manner or by whom, those figures on that cliff were cut and carved, or for what purpose, nor can they see what they mean. Because I myself making a great effort at that very place, which is entrusted to the illustrious gentlemen Francisco de Merida y Molina [book: the illustrious Franciscan council of Merida and Molina (11)], and finding very old men in it, including one who, at the very least, from what we were able to learn there, the religious Father Antonio de Mendoza, (who is alive today and is the definitor of that province of New Spain, the son of the illustrious Luis de Marin, of the most principal conquerors of that world, to whom the province of Guazacalco was entrusted, and of Maria de Mendoza, the aunt of the Count of Aguilar, our highly beloved son in the Lord), was over one hundred forty years old, and I was unable to learn or clarify any more than that it was there from time immemorial, and that it was in his memory and that of his parents and grandparents and progenitors; and the name of the place well shows its antiquity, for as we have said, it was called in their language the moon over the stone, the town being very ancient. But what amazed me the most in such a rare spectacle was that the hue of that most perfect color blue, while exposed to the elements for such a long time, had never faded or gotten worn out."

This marvelous cross still exists today in the same way and the same manner as this author describes it; and some very reliable persons who have seen it have assured me of it, ecclesiastics as well as monks and clerics, who have administered as priests in this sierra as well as lay persons, and among them was one, the Gentleman Boturini, who made a trip to this place for no other purpose than to see and admire this wonder, and he assured me that the spot where it is at is a very high, steep slope of the hill called Tianguistepetl, a climb so eminent and precipitous and so rough that it is not credible that through human strength and industry anyone could have put it there, as it is carved right in the cliff, and its size is a little more than one cubit, on a background of a very fine blue strewn with white stars, and on the right side it has a shield, of the same blue color, with five white balls representing the five very precious wounds of the Lord, the color so permanent that there has been no water, sun, air, nor elements of any kind that have been able to decrease its beauty in any way. Its antiquity is not disputable, for as the author says, explaining the word Meztitlan, this whole sierra took its name from there, and since very ancient times, distant from the coming of the Spanish, it has been called Meztitlan. So this sovereign sign, so admirable for its workmanship, placement, antiquity, and permanence, proves the preaching of the gospel in these countries since the primitive times of Christianity by some apostle or disciple of Christ [book: the Lord] and with its being evident through the histories of the Indians that Quetzalcohuatl was the first who let them know the cross, it is likely that it was this apostle or disciple of the Lord who set it there as a reminder of his preaching, or one of his disciples.

Father Gregorio Garcia himself mentions (12), through the account of another monk of his order, that when the Dominicans entered into the province of the Zapotecs in those early times immediately following the conquest, in a place called Quichapa, they found, in the possession of a chief, a Bible of just figures, which were the characters that served them as letters, the meaning of which they knew, because from fathers to sons, they were teaching how to understand those figures; and they had been keeping this book from a very ancient time; and he also mentions (13) that as Father Alonso de Escalona, of the Order of our Father San Francisco [Saint Francis] was passing through the town of Nejapa, in the province of Huaxaca, the vicar of that convent, who was of the religious order of Santo Domingo, showed him some charts of these Indians of very ancient appearance, which contained some points of our Holy Faith. Among the papers that I have gathered, I have a whole explanation of one of these charts that contains the most principal points of our faith. It begins with the creation of man, his sin, exile from paradise, the flood, the tower of Babel, and this is followed by the incarnation, birth, passion, and death of Christ, and the coming of an apostle who preached the gospel in those early times, and the author of this explanation says that the chart was given to Dr. [book: Bachelor or Graduate] Carlos de Siguenza y G6ngora, who was a very well-known individual in Mexico, where his fame endures today because of his great erudition and knowledge in this subject of antiquities of the Indians, and although I have gathered some of his manuscripts, I haven't been able to have this chart in my hands through the efforts that I have made, curious to see whether or not it is from the ancients; because there are many modern ones, that is, subsequent to the conquest, and these prove nothing, and so I am not using this explanation.

Antonio de Herrera, speaking of the things of Honduras (14), tells of a triangular stone that was found in the land of Cerquin, with three deformed faces on each point, which those natives had in veneration from the most remote antiquity; and although the narration that they gave of how that stone came to be there is fabulous and full of mistakes, it is known that those same fables were invented on the Catholic truths that they knew about in the early centuries, and over the course of time they became distorted, as has happened throughout the world, and this has always been how idolatry has spread and multiplied (Veytia, 157-162).

FOOTNOTES TO CHAPTER XVI

1. I Corinthians 1:23

2. Herrera Dec. 2, book 3, chapter I

3. Gomara 2, c. 15

4. Torquemada 3, book 15, chapter 49.

5. Book 5, chapter 4.

6. Torquemada, 3, book 16, chapter 28.

7. Garcia, Predicaci6n del evangelio, book 5, chapter 5.

8. Brulio, Historia de San Agustin del Peru, book 1, chapter 5.

9. Garcia, Book 5, chapter 6.

10. Calancha, Book 2, chapter 2.

11. It has not been possible to find out what council this might be; and if there is some error here of the copiers, it is not easy to know what it consists of, as it has been difficult to find the book from where the author took this passage.

12. Book 5, chapter 7.

13. Book 5, chapter 8.

14. Dec. 4, book 3, chapter 4.

CHAPTER XVII

The knowledge that they found of the doctrine of Quetzalcohuatl, and the rites and customs that he taught, prove with more efficacy that he was a Holy Apostle.

Besides these vestiges and material signs, others remained from a higher sphere, and they prove with greater efficacy that Quetzalcohuatl was one of the holy apostles or disciples of the Lord, that he preached the gospel in these parts. These are the doctrines, customs, and ceremonies that he taught to these natives, which they preserved in their republics as holy and sacred things, without losing from their memory that it was Quetzalcohuatl who taught them to them. I confirm them in the adoration of the Creator God only, for as we have already said, around these times idolatry had not yet arisen in these countries, and Tloque Nahuaque, or Creator God, was the only object of their adoration, although devoid of all outward worship, because there were no temples, nor did they worship him with outward ceremonies, or sacrifices, or incense, or prayers, so that it was just a knowledge or awareness that all things, and they themselves, were works of the powerful hand of this supreme entity who created them and preserves them, but without their rendering him homage or thanks in any way for these benefits.

Quetzalcohuatl taught them to pray in places separate from all domestic use and intended only to congregate there to worship the Creator God with humility and praises, and to eat together there on certain days, instructing them in the modesty and composure that they should have, and putting the Holy Cross in some of them as a visible object of their adoration, as a figure of the crucified, an instrument of the redemption and a standard that publishes the triumph of the Redeemer. He gave them the knowledge of the ineffable mystery of the Sublime Trinity, explaining to them with those examples and figures provided in their crudeness, such as the triangular stones with the equal and very large faces like the one at Cerquin; and until the arrival of the Spanish in these countries, the memory of the doctrine of Quetzalcohuatl about this mystery was preserved, for as the Bishop of Chiapa, Bartolome de las Casas, mentions in the manuscript that I have already mentioned and which is also referred to by Gregorio Garcia in his work of the Preaching of the Gospel in the New World, (1) and Antonio Remesal in the History of his Province of Dominicos de San Vicente de Chiapa, (2) in Yucatan a principal Indian was found who said, when asked about his ancient religion and beliefs and that of his compatriots, that they believed that there was a Supreme God in Heaven, that although he was just one, there were three persons. They called the first one Izona, and attributed the creation of all things to him; they called the second Bacab, whom they said was the son of Izona, and had been born of a Virgin names Chibirias, who is with God in the heavens; and the third they called Echuah. Eupoco had Bacab whipped, put a crown of thorns on him, and finally, stretched out and tied to a wood, he took his life. He was dead three days, and then resurrected and rose to the heavens with his father. Afterwards Echuah came to the earth and filled it with whatever was needed. He also said that this doctrine was taught by the lords to his children, and that they had a tradition that it was taught by some men who came to those lands in very ancient times, twenty in number, of whom the main one was named Cocolcan; that they wore beards, long clothing, and sandals on their feet; and that these same people taught them to confess and to fast.

The authority of the bishop of Chiapa who gives this report is very respectable; and although he mentions the narration of a certain cleric named Francisco Hernandez, to whom he gave a particular charge to investigate and find out well as much as possible regarding the ancient religion and belief of these natives, we must suppose that he did so with diligence, and at least that he wouldn't feign this fable. Besides the fact that this report is confirmed in Herrera, Salazar, and others, although with some variation, but they all agree that they believed in the existence of a God in three persons, of whom one became man and was born of a virgin, and that this doctrine was taught to them by Cocolcan and his disciples, and this is sufficient for my intent.

Salazar, speaking of the names that they gave to the three persons, believes that with time or because of mispronunciation they were altered and corrupted, and that they were mistaken in the names of the first and second person, because Bacab, which was the name they gave the second, he believes is a corruption of Abba, which means Father; Izona, which was the name they gave the first, he thinks is a corruption of Icon, which means Image, and fits the son better according to St. Paul;(3) and Echuah, which they called the third, seems to be a corruption of Haruach, a Hebrew word that means spirit; and the name of Chibirias or Chiribias that they gave to Our Lady, a corruption of the name of Mary.

Herrera concurs in the coming of Cocolcan and his companions to Yucatan, whom he says came through the west part, three in number, of whom the main one was Cocolcan; but it appears that he puts it many years later, because he says that all three having reigned in Izamal and afterwards founded the city of Mayapan, (4) Cocolcan returned to Mexico, where he had gone by the same road, and there may be a mistake in this, either in those who gave the report or in those who took it, for it could very well have been, and it agrees with the histories of the Indians, that Cocolcan, whom I suppose to be the same as Quetzalcohuatl, for the reasons that I will give later on, or some disciple of his, preached in the settlements of the Olmecs and Xicalancas, which fall to the west with respect to Yucatan, which location was, as we have said, where the territory of Tlaxcallan was later, on the boundary of what was also later the Texcocan empire and kingdom of Mexico; which was not founded until many years later.

Saying that Cocolcan reigned in Izamal should be understood as the respect and veneration with which they looked at him, obeying his precepts with regard to the doctrine and teaching that he gave them, not because in reality he was a king or ruled as such; and this is known with evidence, because they agree in that he was a newcomer and not a native of the country, that he came teaching this doctrine, and afterwards went on to found Mayapan, and so he left them inhabited and educated, he went away, and then they say that he chose one from the lineage of the Cocomes to govern them; that is and should be understood, not as a family known by this name, but of the disciples of Cocolcan, because Cocome is the plural of Cohuatl, or Cocolcan, as we will say later; and thus it means that they chose one of those disciples or followers of Cocolcan to govern them, that they followed and practiced [book: they continued practicing] his doctrine, until these lords or their successors to whom they gave the same name became corrupt and yielded to greed and ambition; which is a very common thing experienced among men at every step, who easily degenerate from the good and sink into evil.

The uses, customs, and ceremonies that were found established throughout New Spain, which by very ancient tradition had to have been introduced by Quetzalcohuatl, are so many and so universal that they alone were sufficient to prove that this was an evangelical preacher who, from those primitive times, instructed them in the law of grace. The knowledge that was found among all these peoples is constant and uniform that he was the one who taught them the forty-day fast that they should observe annually, mortification and penitence, disciplining the back, arms, and calves with burrs and thorns until shedding blood. He exhorted them to give alms and to succor the needs of their neighbor, making them understand that not only should they do so as an act of humanity, but of religion, for love of God and as his gift, without exception of persons; and on this subject there was a festival that was very particular that the Mexicans would celebrate in the month of Hueytecuilhutl in honor of one of their deities named Xilomen, goddess of the tender corn. In it the kings and lords, as well as the other rich gentlemen, would give many poor people food to eat. Not only did it let them know the virtues, but also the vices, seeking to inspire in them hate for the vices, and love for the virtues; and thus, although at the time that he appeared in these regions they already had some manner of government in their republics, more or less, as some nations had become more polished than others, and in general they all had chiefs or lords who commanded them and whom they obeyed and were subject to, who would punish some crimes, many others were left unpunished, because they weren't yet known among them as such, until Quetzalcohuatl let them know, inspiring a great horror in them not only of murder, theft, and the rest which, being prohibited by the natural law, are known by all peoples and nations, but also adultery, lying, unchastity, and drunkenness, persuading them that each man should not have more than one wife, and each woman more than one man, and that once united, they could not separate; and some say that the ceremonies that they used in their marriages, which I will explain later on, were taught to them by Quetzalcohuatl. He also taught them together in a place separated from all bustle and trade to pray and ask the Creator God for the remedy of all their needs, and to go to that place whenever they found themselves afflicted, venerating it as sacred, from which the erection of their temples originated, for the care and assistance of which he instituted priests, whom he instructed in the modesty and composure of truth and circumspection with which they should conduct themselves to be the teachers, directors, and exemplars of the rest. They also assert that in some places he erected schools of virgins, and that those that were found in Mexico and Texcoco, on the arrival of the Spanish, had been erected and were still in existence under the rule or institute that Quetzalcohuatl ordered.

FOOTNOTES TO CHAPTER XVII

1. Garcia, book 5, chapter 9.
2. Remesal, book 5, chapter 7.
3. 2 Corinthians 4:4, and Colossians 1:13.
4. Mayapan was the principal city in Yucatan, the language of which peninsula was named Maya by the Spaniards (Veytia, 163-166).

CHAPTER XVIII

Of other customs and rites that were found established in these countries when the Spanish arrived in them.

Other customs and rites were still found among these peoples at the time of the arrival of the Spanish, which, because of being more particular and characteristic of Christianity, prove more effectively that the person who introduced them was an apostle or disciple of Jesus Christ. Baptism is the first sacrament necessary, without which there can be no salvation, and therefore they rightly call it the door of the Catholic Church, to which no one can enter except by it; and it is evident that throughout this country a type of baptism was found to be established. Although it varied in the ceremonies according to the places, substantially they all agreed on this bath of natural water, saying upon the baptized person some forms such as honors and prayers and putting a name upon him, and this they observed as a rite of religion, preserving the memory of Quetzalcohuatl's having taught it to them. Father Remesal affirms that the first Spanish who arrived at Yucatan found that those natives used a type of baptism, to which they gave a name in their language which in our language means being born again. An expression more in agreement with that of Christ in the Gospel cannot be given. They had (he says) so much devotion and reverence for it that no one failed to receive it. They thought that in it they were receiving a pure disposition to be good and to not be harmed by the devils, and to attain the glory that they were hoping for. It was given to them from the age of three years up until twelve, and without it no one got married. They would choose a day for it that was not one of their tragic days, the fathers would fast for three days beforehand and would abstain from the women, the priests would handle the purification of the home, casting out the devil with certain ceremonies, and once these ceremonies were over the children would go one by one, and the priests would give them a little corn and ground incense in the hand, and they in a brazier, and in a cup they would send wine outside the town, with an order to the Indians not to drink it or look back, (1) and with this they believed that they had cast out the devil. The priest would come out dressed in long, solemn clothing with a hyssop in his hand. They would put white cloths on the heads of the children, they would ask the big ones if they had done any sin, and in confessing they would remove them to a place and bless them with prayers, making movements as if to strike them with the hyssop, and with certain water that they had in a bone, they would wet the forehead and the features of the face and between the toes and the fingers, and then the priest would get up and remove the cloths from the children, and certain notifications being done, they were thus baptized and the festival would end in banquets, and in the nine following days the father of the child was not to approach his wife.

In the territories of Texcoco, Mexico, Tlacopan, Culhuacan, and other regions there were certain festivities in which the ceremony was solemnly done of bathing the children and putting names upon them; but when these festivities were not immediate, it was a custom to bathe the children seven days after they were born, standing them on their feet and throwing water on them from the top of the head, and at the same time they would put the name upon them. If it was a boy, they would put an arrow in the right hand and a target in the left, and if it was a girl, in one hand the spindle and in the other the shuttle, or a broom; and two months after birth (which was after forty days), (2) because each month of theirs was twenty days long, the mothers would take them to present them at the temple, where they were received by one of the priests who was the one who was in charge of keeping the count of their calendar or ecclesiastical chart. This priest would present the child to one of their gods as it seemed right to him, and as a surname would give the child the name of that deity, (3) to whom he did certain honors, and they amounted to asking him to give that child a good and peaceful nature, that it not be hard for him to learn what he should learn, for him to be happy in war, for him not to suffer travails and need, and other similar things.

In some towns their bath was not until the tenth day after birth, and in others it was not by infusion but by immersion, submerging the children in ponds, rivers, springs, or fonts full of water; but in all parts they gave them a name in doing this ceremony of the bath; and although in some parts the remembrance had already been lost of the one who introduced these ceremonies or many of them among them, and among the better educated people, as I have said, the knowledge was found that it was Quetzalcohuatl who taught them this ablution or bath of natural water and to give the children a name at the time of performing it; and it seems natural that being an apostle or disciple of the Lord he would carry it out that way, to fill the commandment that the Lord gave to all his apostles when he commanded them to preach the Gospel throughout all the world and to every creature, baptizing them in the name of the Father, of the Son, and of the Holy Ghost, promising eternal salvation through faith and baptism: Whosoever believes and is baptized shall be saved.

Father Torquemada (4) attained the knowledge of this ceremony of the baptism of children, although not as the Indian writers mention it, because he says that it was done four days after the infant was born, but he agrees in the circumstances that in those four days a fire would burn continuously at the house of the mother who gave birth, with great care that it didn't go out, nor be taken outside the house, because they would say that it would bring harm to the child, and on the fourth day they would pass the baby over the flames, (5) giving this ceremony the name of Tlequiquitzinliztli, which Boturini (6) says they had carried down from their ancestors the descendants of Cham; from which it is inferred that he considered the Indians to be descendants of Cham. This day was one of the most solemn and one with the biggest and most lavish feasts (7) that the principal Lords did, and likewise the poor, each one according to his possibility. He also concurs that at the time of doing this washing or type of baptism, they would give the child a name, (8) and even though before birth or just after the parents would assign the baby a name, they wouldn't name him with it until the washing ceremony was done; and even though he says that they would do this following the other nations of the world who thus practiced it, and he brings examples from the Romans, Greeks, and Hebrews, even though by the histories of these peoples it can in no way be gathered that at any time they had communication with those nations, there is no reason to believe that they learned it from them, and it seems more likely that it was taught to them by Quetzalcohuatl himself, who instructed them in the other points of the gospel law, as some of their national historians assert.

No less remarkable is the custom that they found established of confessing to the priests, declaring to them those things that they had as sins, and accepting the penitence that the priests would impose upon them; and the obligation that the priests had, not to reveal the sins that were confessed to them, was so rigorous that if they violated this confidentiality they were severely punished even with the penalty of death. (9) All the Indian historians speak in confirmation of this custom, and Herrera says (10) that the same thing was practiced in

Nicaragua, and it is very certain that they did not learn this custom in its full extent from the Greeks and Romans.

That there were priests whose ministry was to offer to the gods the sacrifices and gifts of the people, pray for the people, bless them, care for the temples, reprove vices, live in chastity and be sustained from alms is so well established that without having recourse to the manuscripts of the Indians, all our writers unanimously confirm it. That Quetzalcohuatl was the one who instituted this priestly order, and the first who taught to live in chastity, the men as well as the women who lived a communal life in their monasteries, (11) and they were totally dedicated to the worship of the true God in those early times, and in times after the time of their false deities, not only do the Indian historians say it, but also many of the Spanish, as he also taught them to offer to God the fruits of the earth, flowers, and incense, which custom the Spanish found to be so well established, although the true object of this outward worship was varied and obscured, that even today, restored by the gospel light, they practice it so prolixly that it almost touches on superstition.

There is nothing better known than the offerings that they would make of bread and wine, (12) that is, bread of corn dough because they did not have wheat, and that drink that they used for wine. The Mexicans would celebrate a solemn festival in honor of Centeotl, the God of corn, as it was his bread, and they would do this by forming the body of this God in a human figure of the corn dough in which they would mix some herbs. They would cook it on the day of the feast and take it out in a procession with great solemnity, and around it they would put a large number of pieces from the same dough that the priests would bless with certain formulas and ceremonies, with which they believed that all that dough was converted into the flesh of that God. Once the feast was over, the priests distributed all that bread to the people in very small pieces, and they all ate it, large and small, men and women, rich and poor, who received it with great reverence, humility, and tears, saying that they were eating the flesh of their God, and they would also take it to the sick as for medicine. They would fast the forty [book: four] days beforehand, and they considered it a great sin to eat or drink anything after this bread until a half day had gone by, and they would hide the water from the children so that they wouldn't drink it.(13) This was one of the most solemn festivals that they did, and at the end of it, an elder of authority did a type of sermon, explaining those ceremonies.

No less particular is the other festival that they would make to the great God of heaven, sacrificing a man, whom they would tie to a wooden cross, and there they would kill him with arrow strikes. The next day they would sacrifice another man, putting him on another, lower cross, but not shooting arrows, but rather breaking his legs(14) with a stick. Many other vestiges were found in their worship as well as in their customs, that give evidential proof of the knowledge that these peoples had of the principal mysteries of the Catholic religion, which we will see throughout the discourse of this history. For now, what has been said is sufficient to show that Quetzalcohuatl, to whom they attribute all the instruction of their ceremonial, worship. and religious practices. could not have been other than some apostle or disciple of Jesus Christ, for the combination of so many things, which, although perverted afterwards either by ignorance or by malice. show so much conformity with Christianity in their origin, leads one to believe that their institutor could have been none other; and it isn't surprising that over the course of time, and lacking in teachers or directors, they would corrupt the sound [book: the holy] doctrine that they learned, abusing the ceremonial, and falling into idolatry. In Europe, the center of Christianity, so close to the head of the Church and to the Vicar of Christ, which has been watchful and tireless in preserving the purity of the religion, so many abuses have been introduced imperceptibly that it has been necessary to hold councils to reform them, and in their decrees it is amazing to see the extravagances and errors to which men had allowed themselves to be led and which it has been necessary to correct.

Herrera says that in the provinces of Coazacoalco and lluta, they had the custom of circumcising the boys, and Torquemada says that the same use existed among the Totonacas, and some of our writers want to infer from this that these natives were descendants of the Jews. In their histories I have not found any information on this custom; I just find that in one of their festivals that they celebrate to the honor of their famous god Tlaloc, those who did not have posterity and wanted it would cut a small part of the foreskin that they called Metepoliso, and they would offer it as the sacrifice to this God so that he would give them posterity. But even though the information that these authors give may be true, these natives could have gotten the knowledge of this ceremony from the same Quetzalcohuatl, giving them to understand that this was the sign that God gave to his chosen people, that it might be known among all nations, the posterity of Abraham distinguishing themselves in this way, Abraham having been given the promises of the future redemption, which should take place with the coming of the Messiah, who was to be born from his own lineage. He would also let them know that the Messiah himself submitted to this law of circumcision to establish the fulfillment of his promises. And so they could have adopted the use of this ceremony, either out of vanity and a type of nobility to distinguish themselves from other nations, or out of superstition, or through ignorance, after Quetzalcohuatl departed from them, for the governance of the religion having been left in the hands of their priests, the priests would do what they did in other places, and that was to invent new rites, ceremonies, and tricks with which to make themselves respectable and deceive the people, immersing them in an abyss of errors, with which, the true worship being perverted, it degenerated into idolatry. But neither from circumcision nor from other customs in which they are like the Hebrews is it inferred that they descended from them, nor that they learned the ceremonies of outward worship from them, as some say, seeking to persuade that at various times some Hebrews came to these parts, for in their history there is no remembrance of this, and they just attribute to Quetzalcohuatl the first instruction on the subject of religion, worship, and morality. And proof of my opinion on this subject is what Torquemada himself says, that with the little girls they did another indecent ceremony in place of circumcision, and they would not have learned this from the Hebrews, who did not practice it (Veytia, 167-174).

FOOTNOTES TO CHAPTER XVIII

1. It would appear from this passage that the Mexicans felt superstitious scruples about looking back, when the occasion of a person's departing was solemn and important: and it is difficult to imagine (on reading, in the concluding paragraph of the third chapter of the ninth book of Sahagun's History of New Spain, that they not only accounted the act itself unlucky, but believed the person to be a great sinner,) that they were wholly ignorant of the tradition of Lot's wife having been turned into a pillar of salt, as recorded in the twenty-sixth verse of the nineteenth chapter of Genesis.

2. It is extremely remarkable that this was the precise number of days which were to be reckoned, according to the enactment of the twelfth chapter of Leviticus, by Jewish women for the purification after the birth of male children; at the expiration of which period of forty days they presented themselves and their sons with the gifts at the temple, when an atonement was made for the women by the sacrifice of a lamb and a pigeon -or, if she was poor, of two pigeons; after which offering she became clean.

3. Echevarria seems to have been led into error here from not recollecting that Tezcatlipoca and the goddess Chalchiuitliene were adored by the Mexicans under many names. It deserves likewise to be noticed that the Mexicans were accustomed to give their children the

same name as that of the day on which they were baptized; and the signs of the Mexican calendar having
been considered by some of the Spanish missionaries
objects of religious worship, from the superstitious reverence that the Mexicans entertained towards them,
they might be said in this sense to have named their
children after some particular deity.

4. Book 13, chapter 23.

5. To pass children through the flames was an ancient
   Hebrew custom, as we learn from many passages of
   the Old Testament.

6. Idea de una Nueva Historia General de la America
   Septentrional [Idea of a New General History of North
   America], folio 19.

7. We learn from the fifty-eighth verse of the first chapter
   of Saint Luke, that rejoicings took place on the birth of
   Jewish children. These rejoicings were renewed on the
   eighth day after its birth, when the child was circum-
   cised; whence in all probability originated the value
   which the Jews set on the number eight, which number was equally esteemed by the Mexicans, and conse-
   crated to the purposes of superstition.

8. Baptism under the new law was substituted for circumcision under the old; and each rite in its turn became
   indispensable to salvation. Baptism therefore having
   thus superseded the old rite of circumcision, it is probable that the primitive Christians would have deemed
   it incumbent on them to name their children at the
   time of baptizing them; in this manner conforming
   with the ancient Jewish precedent, -since we learn
   from the fifty-ninth verse of the first chapter of Saint
   Luke that it was a Hebrew custom to name children at
   the time of circumcising them.

9. Confession was a religious rite common both in Peru and Mexico; and it was a custom that prevailed in the earliest ages of the Church, although that point is denied by Protestant writers, who contend that it was a fraud of later times, devised for the purposes of promoting spiritual ambition.

10. Decad. 3, book 4, chapter 7, folio 174, co1. 7 and chapter 12, folio 216, col. 2.

11. The same custom prevailed in Peru.

12. Chicha, the name which the Peruvians gave to their drink-offerings, nearly resembled [Hebrew writing]; the term applied to the Hebrew drink-offerings in the Pentateuch.

13. See Herrera, decad. 3, book 2, chapter 17, folio 91.

14. Crucifixion was a common mode of punishment amongst the ancient Jews, whose penal code annexing the clause "thine eye shall not pity" to some of its enactments, and frequently adjudging criminals to be burnt alive, gave a certain tincture of ferocity to the manners of that people, which was rather heightened than diminished by their being permitted indiscriminately to witness and take a part in public executions, when the sentence to be carried into effect was that of stoning a criminal to death. It is worthy of observation that the refined feelings of modern times are shocked at the bare mention of the Roman ladies going to the theatre to view the combats of gladiators; yet there is something infinitely more revolting in the picture which the imagination forms to itself, of a Hebrew market-place crowded with men, women, and children, all eager to stone an adulterer to death, in order to show themselves zealous followers of the Mosaic law. There was mystery, however, as well as barbarity, in

the crucifixions practiced by the Mexicans; and the custom of breaking the legs of a crucified person on one of the festivals, and leaving him in this manner to die upon the cross, reminds us that the Jews broke the legs of those whom they crucified on the eve of the Sabbath day, out of reverence, as it would appear, for that festival. We shall here transcribe a passage from the tenth chapter of the first part of the inedited [unpublished] History of Torribio de Benavente, which fully confirms the account given above by Echevarria; - the sacrifices described are those of the province of Tlaxca1a: "In another festival they would raise up a man tied to a very high cross, and there they would shoot arrows at him; in another festival they would tie another man lower, and they would kill him with oak-pole rods the length of a fathom with very sharp points, goading him like a bull; and they used almost these same ceremonies and sacrifices in the provinces of Huexocinco, Tepezca, Zacatlate, in the main festivals, because they all considered Acatacht1i, which was the large statue that I have said, as the greatest of their gods."

15. Herrera Dec. 4, book 9, chapter 7, folio 235.

CHAPTER XX

Of two famous prophesies that Quetzalcohuatl made when he preached in Chollolan.

Around this time the city of Chollolan was the most famous and numerous settlement of the land of Anahuac. It was in its greatest height and splendor, and was renowned and applauded for its high tower, which as I have said, its inhabitants had built for the glory of their nation and as a monument to declare to those in the future that this had been the first settlement of the Olmecs, and where the founders of the other settlements of this nation had originated. Its outline was round, having in its plane a little more than a thousand yards of diameter, and it rose in a pyramid shape, we don't know to what height; but undoubtedly it was great, as manifested by the ruins that still remain in our times. Its construction deserved the name of hill better than tower, because it was solid of loose rock and large adobes of earth, one layer of these and another layer of rock pressed and compacted with earth, and the ascent, as perceived from the lower remnant of it (which is what is still in existence in the place and manner in which it was built), seems to have gone around its contour through a type of terrace. In one of the charts that Boturini gathered on maguey paper, this hill is seen drawn in the mentioned pyramid shape, with four divisions that served as landings, and they surrounded everything, with sufficient space to walk around them; they say that outside it was covered with a very hard white mortar, of which no trace has remained to this day.

This tower was situated in the middle of the town, which is on a beautiful and fertile plane, although at the present time the tower or hill is almost outside the town, because of how much the surrounding area has decreased, as because of the inhabitants having gone further north, for traces still remain of how far their settlement extended on the opposite side. The splendor of this city was contributed to more than a little by its having been the first in which it is said that houses were built for its dwellers to live in; because situated on a plane where caves were lacking and there were no slopes in which to carve them out, they were obligated by necessity to seek shelter and defense from the inclemency of the weather. For all these reasons its population was very numerous, and even though nothing is known about their government, they had to have had one to keep such a multitude of people in harmony.

These were the ones whom the Apostle Saint Tomas [suggested by Veytia to be Quetzalcoatl] sought, to instruct them in the gospel truths; and finding such a copious harvest field in this city, they say that he stayed there three months preaching and teaching the new law of Jesus Christ. But the time had not yet come for the holy seed to bear fruit, and so with the saint seeing the rebelliousness and hardness of those hearts difficult to yield up in a short time, and having accomplished his mission, he decided to leave them. But first he predicted to them that the time would come in which all would embrace the new law that he was preaching to them, and that in a year that would be indicated with the hieroglyph of a reed, some white, bearded men would come from the East over the waters of the sea, who would strip them of their dominion of the land, and ruling over all the land, they would make them embrace the law of the gospel; and as signs that this, his prophecy, would be perfectly fulfilled, he made them another one, telling them that a few days after his departure from the city, their famous tower would be destroyed, which happened exactly as he predicted it to them, for eight days after the saint had left the city, a very strong earthquake (1) was felt, which brought down the great tower, the ruins remaining in existence until our days as a perpetual reminder of the event that he announced to them, in several fragments, of which there are two so large that they form two little hills immediately at the main base that was left unmovable, and this is about two hundred yards tall. One can only imagine how much must have been destroyed and ruined by the continuation of so many centuries.

The destruction of this tower was, for these peoples, one of the most memorable events, because of the fame of the tower, as well as Quetzalcohuatl's prediction having been fulfilled in its ruin, [omitted from book: which was a sign that] in the same way the one that he made about the coming of those peoples from the East [omitted from book: would be fulfilled] who would become the lords of the land; and as this prophecy had been made in all the other settlements where he had gone, its fulfillment interested everyone, and since then they were persuaded that the time would come in which it would take effect, and they always waited for its fulfillment.

Therefore, when the Spanish arrived in these parts, they found this knowledge to be constant and uniform throughout all the towns of the New Spain, as all the historians assert unanimously; and it was not a small reason for the happiness of their conquests, for the Indians, firmly believing that the prophecy of Quetzalcohuatl could not fail to be fulfilled, they lost enthusiasm for the defense, and in large part the ease with which a small number of Spanish conquered a multitude of them, as the historians of the conquest mention at every step, must be attributed to this. For although in these times of which I am speaking the great empire of Texcoco had not yet arisen, nor the other monarchies that later occupied these lands, the northern most countries and their maritime coasts were already very populated; there were already many settlements on the coasts of the heart of Mexico to Yucatan, in the kingdom of Peru, and it is evidenced through Toltec history that Quetzalcohuatl traveled through all those settlements of the north, teaching the same doctrine and making the same prophecy to them, the knowledge of which was brought by the founders of those monarchies, and finding it corroborated here with the event of Chollolan, they were more firmly persuaded that some day its fulfillment would arrive, and although time introduced some variation into this also, trying to interpret the prophecy as will be mentioned later on, the substance of it, which boils down to announcing the coming of the white people from the East who would dominate the land, remained constant, as is seen by the histories.

In view of this event, these people formed a high concept of Quetzalcohuatl, and started to honor and venerate his memory by putting into practice many of the doctrines that he had taught them, the observance of which they always maintained without forgetting that it had been Quetzalcohuatl who had taught them to them, although later, in the course of time, they introduced some abuses into them. The main one that they make mention of in these times is the worship of the Holy Cross, for which they built a magnificent temple over the remaining base of their famous tower (2) which the Spanish found still in existence with a wooden cross placed in it; and this is the first temple of which I find a report in the histories of the Indians. Nor before this do I find any information that they worshiped any divinity, nor venerated any material idol, nor recognized any Gods other than Tloque Nahuaque or creator of all things. They gave various names to the Holy Cross; those that I find to be most frequent are these three: Quiahuitziteotl, (3) which means the God of wood; Chicahualizteotl, which is interpreted the strong and powerful God; and Tonacaquahuitl, which is interpreted as God of the rains; but its genuine meaning in the Nahuatl language is the pole of fertility or of abundance, an allegory very particular to this language to mean that through this pole they would attain the rains that fertilized their seed planting; and so this was the most common and general name that they gave it; because Quetzalcohuatl having taught them that this sovereign sign had virtue to attract the rains to their sewn fields, and they having experienced this benefit through it, they worshiped it as a powerful deity to succor them in this need, which was of unique [book: great] importance to them; and its worship having spread afterwards into the other kingdoms and monarchies that were founded subsequently, it was always worshiped and known as the god of the rains, with ignorance perverting the true object of the worship, and this was the reason the conquerors have found such a large number of crosses in these countries.

In successive times, with the Toltec nation dominating, the Chololtecs, who were of the same Olmecs now mixed with the Toltecs, again erected their famous tower, and they say that they made it higher than the first time (4), but it was again ruined one night when they least expected it, with no earthquake, hurricane, nor any other cause to attribute it to preceding its destruction, and so it caused so much terror in them that from that time forth they did not dare to attempt its rebuilding again. On the chart or painting of this tower which I talked about at the beginning of this chapter, an inscription is found in the Mexican language, placed there undoubtedly by those first neophytes who learned how to write in our characters, and applauding the Chololtecs, it says that their ancestors did it to save themselves from another flood. It gives the city the name of Tollan Chollolan, and says that that tower is a precious monument of the Toltec nation; but in reality it was the Olmec nation that built it, and realistically they were also the ones, although now mixed with the Toltecs, who restored it. The author of the inscription adds that the archangel Saint Michael was the one who knocked it down this second time (5), and that some people saw him tear it down. Now it is seen that in those times they neither knew Saint Michael nor had his name even reached their ears; and so even though the information may be true (though I have not found in any other author) of having seen persons in the air tearing it down, we must be persuaded that this expression of the author of the inscription is no more than a pious discourse, founded on the fact that the bishopric of Tlaxcallan, now of the Puebla de los Angeles, is under the guardianship and protection of Saint Michael, who with singular wonders has tried to manifest himself as its protector since the early times of its Christianity (Veytia, 184-188).

FOOTNOTES TO CHAPTER XX (KINGSBOROUGH)

1. Ollin, or the sign of the Earthquake, was dedicated to Quecalcoatl, perhaps on this account.

2. This is a very curious passage, as it is here expressly declared that the famous temple of Cholula, which the Spaniards found in a complete state of preservation on their arrival in the New World, and which, dedicated to Quecalcoatl, was frequented by pilgrims from all parts of New Spain, had been built in honor of the cross, and contained a wooden cross when the Spaniards first visited it.

3. This proper name is compounded of quiahuitl, and

teotl, god, and signifies "the god of rain" an interpretation which Echevarria has erroneously given to Tonacaquahuitl; which latter term being compounded of tonacayo, defined by Molina to be "human body, or our flesh," and qu [illegible] tl or quahuitl, which, according to the same author, signifies "wooden tree or pole," may be interpreted "the tree of life or of our bodies." Don Ferdinand de Alba Ixtlilxochitl, in the first chapter of his History of the Chichimecan Empire, mentions these amongst the names by which the cross was adored in ancient times in New Spain; but as he does not assign its signification to each name separately in the order in which he writes them, but explains their meaning collectively, it is not unlikely that this was the cause of Echevarria confounding the signification of Quiahuitzteotl with that of Tonacaquahuitl.

4. The temple of Cholula, like the temple of Jerusalem, was said to have been twice built; and it is singular that after its second destruction the same superstitious notion should have prevailed about any attempt to rebuild it.

5. This tradition supposed the destruction of the second temple of Cholula to have been a judgement on the people of Cholula for their sins.

Hubert Howe Bancroft
(1832-1918)

Hubert Howe Bancroft wrote extensively of the history of the western part of the United States, of Central America and Mexico.

FROM *The Native Races* V

During the Olmec period, that is, the earliest period of Nahua power, the great Quetzalcoatl appeared. We have seen that in the Popol Vuh and Codex Chimalpopoca this being is represented as the half-divinity, half-hero, who came at the head of the first Nahuas to America from across the sea. Other authorities imply rather that he came later from the east or north, in the period of the greatest Olmec prosperity, after the rival Quinames had been defeated. To such differences in detail no great importance is to be attached; since all that can be definitely learned from these traditions is the facts that Quetzalcoatl, or Gucumatz, was the most prominent of the Nahua heroes, and that his existence is to be attributed to this earliest period known in Mexico as Olmec, but without adistinctive name in the south. Quetzalcoatl was a white, bearded man, venerable, just, and holy, who taught by precept and example the paths of virtue in all the Nahua cities, particularly in Cholula. His teachings, according to the traditions, had much in common with those of Christ in the Old World, and most of the Spanish writers firmly believed him to be identical with one of the Christian apostles, probably St. Thomas. During his stay in this region his doctrines do not seem to have met with a satisfactory reception, and he left disheartened. He predicted before his departure great calamities, and promised to return in a future year Ce Acatl, at which time his doctrines were to be fully accepted, and his descendants were to possess the land. Montezuma is known to have regarded the coming of Cortes and the Spaniards as a fulfillment of this prediction (Bancroft, V:200, 201).

QUETZALCOATL IDENTIFIED AS CHRIST

Bancroft suggested in his chapter on Origin of the Americans:

The native traditions concerning the several culture. heroes of America have also been brought forward by a few writers to show that American civilization was exotic and not indigenous; . . . Although bearing various names and appearing in different countries, the American culture-heroes all present the same general characteristics. They are all described as white, bearded men, generally clad in long robes; appearing suddenly and mysteriously upon the scene of their labors, they at once set about improving the people by instructing them in useful and ornamental arts, giving them laws, exhorting them to practice brotherly love and other Christian virtues and introducing a milder and better form of religion; having accomplished their mission, they disappear as mysteriously and unexpectedly as they came; and finally, they are apotheosized and held in great reverence by a grateful posterity. In such guise or on such mission did Quetzalcoatl appear in Cholula, Votan in Chiapas, Wixepecocha in Oajaca, Zamna and Cukulcan [Kukulcan] with his nineteen disciples in Yucatan, Gucumatz in Guatemala, Viracocha in Peru, Sume and Paye-Tome in Brazil, the mysterious apostle mentioned by Rosales in Chili, and Bochica in Columbia.

"The most celebrated of these are Quetzalcoatl and Votan. The speculations which had been indulged in regarding the identity of these mysterious personages are wild in the extreme. Thus Quetzalcoatl has been identified by some with St. Thomas, by others with the Messiah. . . . Those who support the identity of Quetzalcoatl as being St. Thomas include

Siguenza y Gongora, Luis Becerra Tanco and Boturini (Bancroft V: 22-25).

BANCROFT LISTS ARGUMENTS IDENTIFYING QUETZALCOATL WITH THE MESSIAH

Foremost—as being most modern—among those who have thought it possible to identify Quetzalcoatl with the Messiah, stands Lord Kingsborough. . . . To this point he has devoted an incredible amount of labor and research to give any adequate idea of which would require at least more space than I think, as a question of fact, it deserves (Bancroft, V:26).

Lord Kingsborough presents an elaborate argument including the following few points: "How truly surprising it is to find that the Mexicans, who seem to have been quite unacquainted with the doctrines of the migration of the soul and the metempsychosis, should have believed in the incarnation of the only son of their supreme god Tonacatecutle. For Mexican mythology speaking of no other son of that god except Quecalcoatle, who was born of Chimalman, the Virgin of Tula, without connection with man, and by his breath alone (by which may be signified his word or his will, announced to Chimalman by word of mouth of the celestial messenger, whom he dispatched to inform her that she should conceive a son), it must be presumed that Quecalcoatle was his only son. Other arguments might be adduced to show, that Mexicans believed that Quecalcoatle was both a god and man, that he had previously to his incarnation existed from all eternity, that he had created both the world and man, that he descended from heaven to reform the world by penance, that he was born with the perfect use of reason, that he preached a new law, and, being king of Tula, was crucified for the sins of mankind, as is obscurely insinuated by the interpreter of the Vatican Codex, plainly declared in the traditions of Yucatan, and mysteriously represented in the Mexican paintings" (Kingsborough, VI:507 -508). (See also Bancroft, V:27; Quetzalcoatl's crucifixion and identity with the Messiah).

"Votan, another mysterious personage, closely resembling Quetzalcoatl in many points, was the supposed founder of the Maya civilization. He is said to have been a descendant of Noah and to have assisted at the building of the Tower of Babel. After the confusion of tongues he led a portion of the dispersed people to America. There he established the kingdom of Xibalba and built the city of Palenque" (Bancroft, V:27).

BANCROFT'S THEORIES
ON THE ORIGIN OF NATIVE AMERICANS

Bancroft reviewed numerous theories of the origin of native Americans which present a background for identification of Quetzalcoatl.

"The theory that the Americans are of Jewish descent has been discussed more minutely and at greater length than any other. Its advocates, or at least those of them who have made original researches, are comparatively few; but the extent of their investigations and the multitude of parallelisms they adduce in support of their hypotheses, exceed by far anything we have yet encountered.

"Of the earlier writers on this subject, Garcia is the most voluminous. Of modern theorists Lord Kingsborough stands preeminently first, as far as bulky volumes are concerned, though Adair, who devotes half of a thick quarto to the subject, is by no means second to him in enthusiasm—or rather fanaticism—and wild speculation" (Bancroft, 5:77-78).

Bancroft gave in some detail "the account given by the Book of Mormon, of the settlement of America by the Jews" which he translated "freely from Bertrand, Memoires, 32, et seq."

Briefly he tells the story of the first inhabitants in America, as related in the Book of Mormon, who came after the Biblical related confusion of tongues. This civilization flourished and died. A second group came from Jerusalem in the first year of the reign of Zedekiah, king of Judah. Shortly after their arrival in America they separated themselves into two distinct nations. One group was called Nephites and the other was called Lamanites. After about 600 years there occurred a most significant event, Christ visited the Nephites in America. Bancroft described it.

"The Nephites were informed of the birth and death of Christ by certain celestial and terrestrial phenomena, which had long before been predicted by their prophets. But in spite of the numerous blessings which they had received, they fell at length from grace, and were terribly punished for their ingratitude and wickedness. A thick darkness covered the whole continent; earthquakes cast mountains into valleys; many towns were swallowed up, and others were destroyed by fire from heaven. Thus perished the most perverse among the Nephites and Lamanites, to the end that the blood of the saints and prophets might no longer cry out from the earth against them. Those who survived these judgments received a visit from Christ, who, after his ascension [in Palestine], appeared in the midst of the Nephites. in the northern part of South America. His instructions, the foundation of a new law, were engraved on plates of gold, and some of them are to be found in the Book of Mormon; but by far the greater part of them will be revealed only to the saints, at a future time.

"When Christ had ended his mission to the Nephites, he ascended to heaven, and the apostles designated by him went to preach his gospel throughout the continent of America. In all parts the Nephites and Lamanites were converted to the Lord, and for three centuries they lived a godly life. But toward the end of the fourth century of the Christian era, they returned to their evil ways, and once more they were smitten by the arm of the Almighty. A terrible war broke out between the two nations, which ended in the destruction of the ungrateful Nephites. Driven by their enemies towards the north and north-west, they were defeated in a final battle near the hill of Cumorah, in the State of New York, where their historical tablets have been since found. Hundreds of thousands of warriors fell on both sides. The Nephites were utterly destroyed with the exception of some few who either passed over to the enemy, escaped by flight, or were left for dead on the field of battle. Among these last were Mormon and his son Moroni, both upright men. Mormon had written on tablets an epitome of the annals of his ancestors, which epitome he entitled the Book of Mormon. At the command of God he buried in the hill Cumorah all the original records in his possession, and at his death he left his own book to his son Moroni, who survived him by some years, that he might continue it. Moroni tells us in his writings that the Lamanites eventually exterminated the few Nephites who had escaped the general slaughter at the battle of Cumorah, sparing those only who had gone over to their side. He himself escaped by concealment. The conquerors slew without mercy all who would not renounce Christ. Finally, he adds that his work is a complete record of all events that happened down to the year 420 of the Christian era, at which time, by divine command, he buried the Book of Mormon in the hill of Cumorah, where it remained until removed by Joseph Smith, September 22, 1827" (Bancroft, V:96-102). (See also, Book of Mormon in Appendix.) Bancroft related in a footnote concerning certain gold plates and an instrument called Urim Thummin (Exodus 28:30; Leviticus 8:8) which were found on the side of the Hill Cumorah by Joseph Smith, as he was led there and given instruction by a heavenly messenger. The Hill Cumorah is near the village of Manchester, Ontario County, State of New York (Ibid., 102). (See also Pearl of Great Price, Joseph Smith-History 1:51-55.)

William Hickling Prescott
(1796- 1859)

Prescott was an American historian writing chiefly of the Conquistadores, famous for his two volumes, History of the Conquest of Mexico (1843), and The Conquest of Peru (1847) We shall quote chiefly here from his History of the Conquest of Mexico. After discussing some of the beliefs of the Aztecs he commented:

But none of the deities of the country suggested such astonishing analogies with Scripture, as Quetzalcoatl. . . . He was the white man, wearing a long beard, who came from the East; and who, after presiding over the golden age of Anahuac, disappeared as mysteriously as he had come, on the great Atlantic Ocean. As he promised to return at some future day, his reappearance was looked for with confidence by each succeeding generation. There is little in these circumstances to remind one of Christianity. But the curious antiquaries of Mexico found out, that to this god were to be referred the institution of ecclesiastical communities, reminding one of the monastic societies of the Old World; that of the rites of confession and penance; and the knowledge even of the great doctrines of the Trinity and the Incarnation! One party, with pious industry, accumulated proofs to establish his identity with the Apostle St.Thomas [one of the twelve apostles selected and ordained by Jesus of Nazareth]; while another, with less scrupulous faith, saw, in his anticipated advent to generate the nation, the type, dim-veiled, of the Messiah!" (Prescott, 695).

The missionaries who first landed in this world of wonders . . . were astonished by occasional glimpses of rites and ceremonies, which reminded them of a purer faith. . . . They could not suppress their wonder, as they beheld the Cross, the sacred emblem of their own faith, raised as an object of worship in the temples of Anahuac [Mexico]. They met with it in various places; and the image of a cross may be seen at this day, sculptured in bas-relief, on the walls of the buildings of Palenque, while a figure bearing some resemblance to that of a child is held up to it, as if in adoration (Ibid., 695).

Their surprise was heightened, when they witnessed a religious rite which reminded them of the Christian communion. On these occasions, an image of the tutelary deity [guardian god, Huitzilopochtli] of the Aztecs was made of the flour of maize, mixed with blood, and, after consecration by the priests was. distributed among the people, who, as they ate it, 'showed signs of humiliation and sorrow, declaring it was the flesh of the deity!' How could the Roman Catholic fail to recognize the awful ceremony of the Eucharist [Sacrament of the Lord's Supper]?

With the same feelings they witnessed another ceremony, that of the Aztec baptism; in which, after a solemn invocation, the head and lips of the infant were touched with water, and a name was given to it; which the goddess Ciocoatl, who presided over childbirth, was implored, "that the sin, which was given to us before the beginning of the world, might not visit the child, but that, cleansed by these waters, it might live and be born anew!" (Ibid., 696).

It is true, these several rites were attended with many peculiarities, very unlike those in any Christian church. But the fathers fastened their eyes exclusively on the points of resemblance . . . (Ibid., 697).

The Jewish and Christian schemes were strangely mingled, and the brains of the good fathers were still further bewildered by the mixture of heathenish abominations, which were so closely intertwined with the most orthodox observances. In their perplexity, they looked on the whole as the delusion of the Devil, who counterfeited the rites of Christianity and the traditions of the chosen people, that he might allure his wretched victims to their own destruction.

Although it is not necessary to resort to this startling supposition, nor even to call up an apostle from the dead, or any later missionary to explain the coincidences with Christianity, yet these coincidences must be allowed to furnish an argument in favor of some primitive communication with that great brotherhood of nations on the old continent, among whom similar ideas have been so widely diffused (Ibid., 691-698).

Edward King Kingsborough

Edward King Kingsborough (Lord), (1795-1837) an Englishman of royalty, believed that the Native America (Indians) were of Israel, part of the lost ten tribes. He collected nine volumes of "Antiquities of Mexico"—relics, paintings, and writings of early Mexico. They were published in England, 1831-1848. Some of his comments on Quetzalcoahtl follow from chapter 24 of Torquemada, Indian Monarchy.

Quetzalcohautl signifies The Feathers of the Serpent or the Feathered Serpent; and this kind of serpent, the name of which these Indians bestowed on their god, is found in the province of Xacalanco, which borders on the kingdom of Yucatan, on the road from that of Tabasco. This god Quetzalcohuatl was greatly celebrated by the inhabitants of the city of Cholulla, and esteemed in that place as the greatest of their gods. They record that he was a white man, tall in stature, with a broad forehead, long and black hair, and a large and round beard" (Kingsbor-ough, VI: 258-259).

"They likewise praise him for his chastity and uprightness, and his exceeding temperance. This god was held in such veneration and reverence, and his shrine was so frequented and honored with vows and pilgrimages throughout all those kingdoms, on account of his peculiar attributes. . . . for in truth the dominion of Quetzalcohuatl was sweet, and he exacted no service from them but easy and light things instructing them in such as were virtuous and prohibiting such as were wicked, evil and injurious, teaching them likewise to abhor them" (Ibid., 260-261).

He had priests who were called Quetzalcohua, which appellation signifies religious persons and priests of the order of

Quetzalcohuatl. . . . They say that this god Quetzalcohuatl, whilst in this mortal life, wore long vests reaching to the feet from a sense of decency, with a mantle above interspersed with red crosses (Ibid. 261).

Kingsborough quoted Sahagun's History of New Spain about the ancient Tultecas:

They were very religious and much addicted to prayer; they worshiped only one Lord, whom they considered God, and they named him Quetzalcoatl, whose priest bore likewise the same appellation, being also named Quetzalcoatl, who was very devout and zealous in the service of the lord his God, and on that account held in great veneration by them; so that whatever he commanded them to do they did, without failing in any part of their obedience to him; he was accustomed frequently to declare that there was one only God and Lord, whose name was Quetzalcoatl, and that he required no other sacrifices but snakes and butterflies" (Ibid, VI:371).

Kingsborough gave reasons for supposing that Christians in early ages colonized America:

"It is so singular a fact that the Indians of Mexico and Peru should have believed with Christians in many doctrines which are held to be peculiarly and exclusively Christian, and to constitute a line of demarcation between Christianity and all other religions, that it appears a convincing proof that Christianity must in early ages have been established in America, and that ancient communications subsisted between the old and new continent at a period long antecedent to the age of Columbus.

In pointing out some of the leading doctrines of Christianity, the knowledge of which was likewise found amongst the Indians, it may be proper to observe, that although it might be easily shown that the Indians believed in the existence of the Deity, in the immorality of the soul, and in a future state of rewards and punishments; still as these are intuitive truths which all religions teach, which all ages have believed, no inferences will be attempted to be drawn from them; since the Romans or the Greeks, the Mahometans or the Hindoos, might by the same arguments be proved to have carried on intercourse in former ages with the Indians.

The doctrines more peculiarly Christian, a belief in which the Indians likewise professed, however mixed up with other superstitions, and from which inferences may be fairly drawn, are the following: That of a Trinity, of original sin, of repentance and penance, of a vicarial atonement, of a future redeemer, and of the resurrection of the body. But, besides exhibiting a certain degree of conformity on these doctrinal points, they likewise seem to have been formerly acquainted with the sacraments, although superstition had lamentably perverted these ancient mysteries of the Christian Church, since traces of them may be found in various rites and ceremonies common alike to the Mexicans and Peruvians. Having briefly mentioned what the particular doctrines of Christianity were, which the gravest writers assert were known to the Indians before the arrival of the Spaniards in the New World, we shall proceed separately to adduce proofs to show that the above-mentioned doctrines did in reality constitute a portion of the Indian faith; and although many testimonies from different authors might be cited in confirmation of each article it will be sufficient in this place to quote the single authorities of men like Acosta, Peter Martyr, Garcia and Torquemada, whose writings are highly appreciated in Spain, and are also known to the rest of Europe (Ibid., 409-410).

And first with respect to the doctrine of a Trinity. Acosta says that the belief of the Peruvians was as follows; (Ibid., 410-411) his words, as far as the Latin translation by De Bry may be supposed to be correct, are these: `that which is here most worthy of remark, is the fact that Satan, in order to increase the majesty of his own worship, has wished by cunningly introducing the doctrine of the Holy Trinity among the Indians, to abuse it; for they have given these names to the three above-mentioned images of the sun, Apointi, Churiunti, and Intiquaoqui; the significations of which are, The Father and Lord of the sun, the Son, the sun itself, and the Brother of the sun. They bestowed the same appellations also on Chuquella, that is, the god whose habitation they supposed was in that tract or region of the air whence proceed thunder, rain and snow, as they had done on the three images. In Chuquisaca an idol was once shown to me to which the Indians were accustomed to pray: they called Tangatanga, and believed it to be a god who was one in three, and three in one" (Acosta, V:xxviii).

It is not known with certainty that the annunciation of the Gospel had crossed over to enlighten the people of America before that continent became known to the Spaniards. If any thing is calculated to produce astonishment, it is the particular belief which the Indians of Yucathan, above all the other nations of these extensive kingdoms, entertained; which renders it at least very difficult to comprehend how that was possible, without the mysteries of the evangelical law having been preached to them; in proof of which I shall cite what Father Remesal relates in his History.

He affirms then, that when the Bishop Don Bartholomew de las Casas proceeded to his bishoprick, which as has been observed in the third book was in fifteen hundred and forty-five, he commissioned an ecclesiastic whom he found in Campeche, whose name was Francis Hernandez, (who is the person who is mentioned in the chapter which treats of the foundation of the city of Merida and in other chapters,) who was well acquainted with the language of the Indians, to visit them, carrying with him a sort of catechism of what he was about to preach to them; and that nearly at the end of a year the ecclesiastic wrote to him that he had met with a principal lord, who, on being questioned respecting the ancient religion which they professed, told him that they knew and believed in the God who was in heaven, and that this God was the Father, Son, and Holy Ghost, and that the Father was named Yzona, who had created men; and that the Son was called Bacab, who was born of a virgin of the name of Chiribirias, and that the mother of Chiribirias was named Yxchel; and that the Holy Ghost was called Echvah.

Of Bacab, the Son, they said that he was put to death, and scourged and crowned with thorns, and placed with his arm extended upon a beam of wood, to which they did not suppose that he had been nailed, but that he was tied, where he died, and remained dead during three days, and on the third day came to life and ascended into heaven, where he is with his Father; and that immediately afterwards Echvah, who is the Holy Ghost, came and filled the earth with whatsoever it stood in need of. Being asked what signification he assigned to the three names of the three persons, he said, that Yzona signified the great Father, and Bacab the Son of the great Father, and Echvah the Merchant. Chiribirias he understood to mean the mother of the son of the great Father. He further added, that all mankind would in course of time perish; but they knew nothing of the resurrection of the flesh. Being questioned likewise as to the manner in which they became acquainted with these things, he replied that the lords instructed their sons in them, and that thus the doctrine was handed down from generation to generation. They declared that in ancient times twenty men had come to that country, the chief of whom was named Cozas, who commanded the people to use confession, and to fast, for which reason some of them fasted on the day corresponding to Friday, affirming that Bacab had been put to death on that day."

Cogolludo further observes in the same chapter of his History of Yucatan, that other circumstances besides their religious creed induced the Dominicans to believe that Christianity had been preached to the inhabitants. . . . t is to be regretted that the same writer has to record in the following terms the extensive destruction of ancient monuments and paintings which immediately followed the arrival of the first Spanish missionaries in Yucatan, which it is to be presumed would have thrown some light on the history of its ancient colonization by Cozas and his companions, whose name bears some semblance to Cozoi, the epithet by which the four divine personages of whom the Mexicans entreated rain were designated, from whom he might have received that appellation. "The ecclesiastics of this province, whose care accelerated the conversion of these Indians to our holy Catholic faith, animated with the zeal which they felt for their interests, not only destroyed and burned all the idols which they worshiped, but likewise all the books which they possessed, composed after their peculiar style, by which they were enabled to preserve the memory of past events, and whatsoever else they imagined might furnish occasion for the practice of superstition of any pagan rites.

This is the reason why some particular facts which I wished to notice in this work cannot be ascertained; but even the knowledge of their historical annals has been denied to posterity, for nearly all their histories were committed to flames without any attention being paid to the difference of the matter of which they treated. Neither do I approve of that suggestion, nor do I condemn it; but it appears to me that secular history might have been preserved in the same manner as that of New Spain and of other conquered provinces has been preserved without its being considered to be any obstacle to the progress of Christianity. I shall, however, in consequence, be able to say little more than that which has already been written of their religious usages in the time of paganism" *(Historia de Yucathan, IV:vi).*

If more of the historical paintings and monuments of Yucatan had been preserved, we should probably have been able to have determined whether Bacab and Quecalcoatle were only two different names for the same deity, who was worshiped alike by the Mexicans and the people of Yucatan. Torquemada informs us, on the authority of Las Casas, that Quecalcoatle had been in Yucatan, and was there adored. The interpreter of the Vatican Codex says, in the following curious passage, that the Mexicans had a tradition that he, like Bacab, died upon the cross, and he seems to add, according to their belief, for the sins of mankind: This tradition, which rested solely upon the authority of the anonymous interpreter of that

MS., acquires the most authentic character from the corroboration which it receives from several paintings in the Codex Borgianus, which actually represent Quecalcoatle crucified and nailed to the cross. These paintings are contained in the fourth, seventy-second, seventy-third, and seventy-fifth pages of the above-mentioned MS.; the article of his resurrection, burial, and descent into hell, appears also to be represented in the seventy-first and seventy-third pages of the same MS (Ibid. VI:166).

Kingsborough discussed that the Spaniards taught the Indians of the resurrection of the body and suggested that "on this point, and not on the immortality of the soul, that Christianity differs from the religions of antiquity; and it is very singular that it should have been discovered in the New World. Gomara, after stating that the Peruvians deposited gold and silver vases in the tombs of the Ingas, says: `When the Spaniards opened these sepulchers and scattered the bones, the Indians entreated them not to do so assuring them that they would be united in the resurrection: for they fully believe in the resurrection of the body and in the immortality of the soul.' (*La Istoria de las Indias*, lxix).

Herrera likewise, in several passages of his History of the Indies, asserts that the Indians maintained this belief. He says, in his fourth decade, page 187, `In the provinces of Guazacualco and Yluta they believed that the dead would come to life; and when the bones of such as died among them had dried up they collected them in a basket and hung them to the branch of a tree, that they might be at no loss to find them when the period of the resurrection arrived.' He says also, `In the province of Quimbaya they well knew that there was an immortal principle in man, although they thought that it was not his soul, but a (bodily) transfiguration, believing that the body would be restored to life. They explained further, that its future habitation would be some delightful and pleasant place, and they used interment like the other Indians" (Herrera, 177).

The Mexicans bestowed the appellation of Topiltzin on

Quetcalcoatle, the literal signification of which is "our son" or "our child," that proper name being compounded of "our," and piltzin, defined by Alonso de Molina in his rare and copious vocabulary of the Mexican and Spanish languages, to be nino o nina, "a boy or a girl," and associated by him with the cognate terms of piltontli and piltzintia; and it may not be unreasonably assumed, since analogies, which are numerous and not isolated, as their number increases increase also in their ratio of probability, not only that the Mexicans were acquainted with Isaiah's famous prophecy, but to mark their belief of the accomplishment of that prophecy in the person of Quecalcoatle, that they named him Topiltzin; no less on account of his having been born from a virgin of the daughters of men, than because another equally celebrated prediction of the same prophet declared, that he should receive a name from that very circumstance: "Therefore the Lord himself shall give you a sign, Behold a virgin shall conceive and bear a son, and shall call his name Immanuel" (Isaiah 7:14]). And the proper name Topiltzin does in fact bear a signification corresponding, if not literally, yet entirely in substance with that of Immanuel: since `God with us,' which is the interpretation of the Hebrew name, means God domiciliated amongst men; and the full force of the expression is preserved in the term Topiltzin, which might be interpreted the Son of Man, or God on a level with men; for the Mexicans believed that Quecalcoatle took human nature upon him, partaking of all the infirmities of man, and was not exempt from sorrow, pain, or death, and that he suffered voluntarily to atone for the sins of mankind. They also believed that he alone of all the gods had a human body, and was of a corporeal essence; a notion which we can only wonder whence it could have been revived. Las Casas and Torquemada both assert that Quecalcoatle had been in Yucatan; and there can be little doubt, when we reflect on the mysterious history of Bacab, that the Cross discovered by M. Dupaix in the ancient temple of Palenque was connected with the tradition of his crucifixion (Ibid., 507).

It is singular that the Mexicans should have viewed Quecalcoatle in the light of a god and of a man, of a father and of a son, of the creator of the world and of him by whom the world was finally doomed to be destroyed, since it is hard to reconcile such conflicting notions with each other (Ibid., 508). That they did so, will be apparent from the following passages extracted from the sixth book of Sahagun's History of New Spain, which contains the prayers addressed by the ancient Mexicans to their gods, as well as from what has already been said of the probable derivation of the proper name of Topiltzin, and from what remains to be said in the belief which the Mexicans entertained, that the world would be destroyed when the Sun should be in the sign of four earthquakes. Quecalcoatle is emphatically styled Father in the exhortation which the Mexican priest addresses to the penitent who had come to make confession to him of his sins, whose entire speech will be found at page 359 of the fifth volume of the Antiquities of Mexico. "When thou wert created and sent into this world, thou was created and sent into it pure and good, and thy father and mother Quetzalcoatl formed thee like a precious stone, like a rich jewel of gold, beautiful to look upon and well polished; but thou by thine own free will and choice hast defiled and polluted thyself, and hast wallowed in the mire of the sins and iniquities which thou hast committed, and now thou hast confessed." From this passage it is plain that the doctrine of free will, as opposed to absolute predestination, was a fundamental article of the religion of the Mexicans, although in some degree qualified by their notions on judicial astrology, as we learn from the following passage of the same chapter of the sixth book of Sahagun; where the Mexican priest or confessor, supplicating Tezcatlipoca on the behalf of the repentant sinner, addresses him in the following language; "I am speaking in the presence of Your Majesty who knowest all things, and knowest that this miserable man did not sin with the entire liberty of his free will, since he partly acted under the influence of the sign in which he was born." The notion of the original sin, in the acceptation in which the term is understood by Christians, which was totally different both in cause and quality from the frailty of human nature, which the ancient philosophers were all prepared to admit, was quite familiar to minds of the Mexicans, who ascribed it to Suchiquecal, and to her disobedience in plucking fruit in the garden of Tamoanchan; and hence a difficulty may arise in understanding the construction which ought to be put on that part of the speech of the Mexican priest to the penitent, where he says to him "when thou wert created and sent into this world, thou was created and sent into it pure and good;" which seems merely to allude to what is said in the first chapter of Genesis, of man having been created in the image of God, and of the works of his hands being all good, and to contain no denial of the doctrine of original sin (Ibid., 508).

"That the Mexicans knew that man had been created in the image of God, may be inferred from the following passage of Sahagun, which deserves to be considered in connection with the Peruvian tradition of men having been created by Viracocha after the likeness of images made by himself, which is perhaps after all only a sample of the artifices to which the Spanish clergy had recourse in order to consign to oblivion all knowledge of the ancient religion of Peru; which could more easily and with less suspicion be effected by substituting fables of their own for those of the Peruvians, and modifying the latter as the occasion required, so as to impose even on the recollection of the Indians, than by a rude attempt to banish them wholly from their memory (Ibid.,508-509).

After much discussion Kingsborough continued:

The above mentioned Histories [Herrera, Gomara, Boturini, Peter Martyr, Mendieta, Rosales, Torquemada] all declare that a white man preached among them a holy law, and the fast of forty days, which the Emperor Netzahualcoyotl, in the greatest vicissitudes of his reign, frequently practiced; and they add, that at his departure from them he left a prophecy, that in the year of their calendar, Ce Acatl, One Cane, his sons would come from the East to preach again to them; which was the reason why the Indians were so disturbed at the intelligence of the arrival of the Spaniards exactly in the year and character Ce Acatl. And I, following the track of the Indian calendars, have discovered that the prophecy of the saint was verified to the letter. The Indians, availing themselves of the lofty metaphors of their language, have bestowed the name of Quetzalcohuatl upon the glorious apostle, which signifies 'the serpent-bird,' intimating by the bird, the swiftness with which he had passed from a distant country to theirs; and by the serpent, the wise circumspection of the law which he came to preach, the value of which was further denoted by the feather of the bird, which they called Quetzalli, and infinitely esteemed; since they wore them not only as an ornament in war, but likewise at their public dances and solemn festivals"(Catalogo del Museo Indiano, 51).

With reference to the tradition which Boturini mentions as prevalent in New Spain, of Saint Thomas having preached the Gospel in that part of America, and of the impression of his feet being visible in many places, it may be remarked that that tradition seems to have been general over all America.

Rosales, in his edited *History of Chile*, declares that the inhabitants of that extremely southern portion of America, situated at the distance of so many thousand miles from New Spain, and who did not employ paintings to record events accounted for their knowledge of some of the doctrines of Christianity by saying, "that in former times, as they had heard their fathers say, a wonderful man had come to that country, wearing a long beard, with shoes, and a mantle such as the Indians carry on their shoulders, who performed many miracles, cured the sick with water, caused it to rain, and their crops and grain to grow, kindled fire at a breath, and wrought other marvels, healing at once the sick and giving sight to the blind; and that he spoke with as much propriety and elegance in the language of their country as if he had always resided in it, addressing them in words very sweet and new to them, telling them that the Creator of the universe resided in the highest place of heaven, and that many men and women who were resplendent as the sun dwelt with him.

They say that he shortly afterwards went to Peru, and that many, in imitation of the habit and shoes which that man used, introduced among themselves the fashion of wearing shoes, and the loose mantle over the shoulders, either fastened with a clasp at the breast, or knotted at the corners; whence it may be inferred that this man was some apostle whose name they do not know." This is the account given by Rosales of that wonderful man; and it deserves to be remarked, as quite in accordance with the gloomy and misanthropical character with which the Indians loved to invest religion, that they converted an object of reverence into one of horror, by assigning to him the attribute of breathing fire from his nostrils" (Ibid., VI:419).

Kingsborough discussed Mexican paintings as found in his Mexican Antiquities:

As in the tradition current in Yucatan of Bacab and his crucifixion (which both Remesal and Torquemada have recorded, the latter on the authority of Las Casas himself, and which it deserves particularly to be noticed, each author has accompanied with some new circumstance in his relation, Remesal informing us that the name of the respectable ecclesiastic who gave the information to Las Casas was Francis Hernandez, and Torquemada that it was Eopuco who scourged and put to death Bacab), so in these Mexican paintings many analogies may be traced between the events to which they evidently relate, and the history of the crucifixion of Christ as contained in the New Testament. The subject of them all is the same—the death of Quecalcoatle upon the cross, as an atonement for the sins of mankind. In the fourth page of the Borgian MS., he seems to be crucified between two persons in the act of reviling him who hold, it appears, halters in their hands, the symbols perhaps of some crime for which they were themselves going to suffer.

It is very remarkable that, although Quecalcoatle strictly enjoined honesty, temperance, and chastity to the Mexicans, he still should have been esteemed by thieves as their patron god.". . . In the seventy-second page of the Borgian MS., Yztapal Nanazcaya, or the fourth age of the Mexicans, that of Flints and Canes, memorable for being the era of the birth of Quecalcoatle and of the destruction of the province and city of Tulan, seems to be represented. Quezalcoatle is there painted in the attitude of a person crucified, with the impression of nails both in his hands and feet, but not actually upon a cross, and with the image of death beneath his feet, which an angry serpent seems threatening to devour. . . . The body of Quecalcoatle seems to be formed out of a resplendent sun, and two female figures with children on their backs are very conspicuously presenting an offering at his feet. The Mexican sometimes added the epithet of Tlatzolli to Tzonpantli, when the signification of both names became, the Place of precious death or martyrdom; tlatzolli meaning in the Mexican language, precious or desired.

The seventy-third page of the Borgian MS. is the most remarkable of all, for Quecalcoatle is not only represented there as crucified upon a cross of the Greek form, but his burial and descent into hell are also depicted in a very curious manner; his grave, which is somewhat in the shape of a cross, and strewed with bones and skulls symbolical of death, resembles likewise that kind of building which the Indians of New Spain constructed in the courts of their temples, which they called tlacho, and in which they played the religious game of the ball, instituted perhaps in commemoration of him. The head of the devouring monster on the left signifies his descent into hell, and that he had been swallowed up in death, which could only dismember, but could not cause his body wholly to corrupt or decay away, since he reassumes his perfect form in hell and seems to compel Mictlantecutli, the lord of the dead, to do him homage.

. . . Quecalcoatle is again represented as crucified in the seventy-fifth page of the Borgian MS., and one of his hands and both his feet seem to bear the impressions of nails; he appears from the phonetic symbol placed near his mouth to be uttering an exclamation, and his body is strangely covered with suns. . . . The seventy-first page of the same MS. seems to represent a cross overshadowed by the wings of a cherub, beneath which Quecalcoatle is reclining, whilst the figures of the sides and the mutilated human limbs around, may bear some allusion to the punishment of his enemies. The eagles which are represented in the same page, remind us that that bird is sometimes mentioned in the Old Testament as an instrument of divine wrath, as in the eleventh verse of the forty-sixth chapter of Isaiah.

WHO WAS QUETZALCOATL?

One lingering question that remains when one reads of the traditions of the Indians: Who was Quetzalcoatl, Kuklkulcan, Viracocha, he whom many claim taught the Indians the traditions to which they were so closely bound? Was he St. Thomas, one of the twelve apostles of Jesus of Nazareth, or some other missionary? According to Hammond and Willey:

Quetzalcoatl-Kukulcan in the form of Venus was worshiped at various centers on the East Coast, [of Yucatan], such as Tulum, Tancah, and Xelha. He was the Pre-Columbian deity who was said to have died as a mortal and, as Venus, or Morning Star, was supposed to come again, rising out of the eastern sea after a period in the underworld. The sixteenth-century Spanish friars preaching the essential mystery of Christian faith—"Christ has died. Christ has risen. Christ will come again"—could well have received a nod of recognition from the Maya. Certainly the concept of resurrection was far from alien to Maya cosmoslogy. And the traditional east—west orientation of Christian churches, including the Tancah chapel, could have been interpreted as further evidence of the Kukulcan-Christ identification.

We cannot say for certain that the East Coast Maya or any other Mesoamerican group accepted Christianity as the fulfillment of the Quetzalcoatl-Kukulcan prophecies. However, there is enough resemblance between the symbolism and dogma of the two cults to help account for the receptivity to Christianity on the East Coast and elsewhere"

(Hammond and Willey, 239-240).

In the Maya vocabulary, many words correspond with those in the English language relating to the Christian faith. A few are listed here (Willard, 134):

God	KU
heaven	CAAN
god of death	AHPUCH
hell	METNAL
sin	KEBAN
Lucifer, prince of devils	XIBALBA
venial sin	ZAL-KEBAN
soul	PIXAN or OL
purge the soul	HALAB-OL
virgin	ZUHUY
love	YACUNAH
sermon	TZEC
converted soul	CI-OL
priest's seat or throne	KUL-XEC
cross	U-AHOM-CHE
to baptize and be born again	CAPUT -ZIHIL
false prophet	EZ-BIL-UINIC

IT WAS ALL OF THE DEVIL

Some recognizing the obvious similarities to Christianity refused to accept the idea that America was evangelized by an early missionary. They attributed all to the Devil.

Wrote Duran, "Once an old Indian woman, wise in the ancient ways, perhaps a former priestess, was brought to me. She told me that in ancient times the natives had an Easter, Christmas, and Corpus Christi, just as we do, and on the same dates, and she pointed out other very important native feasts which coincide with our celebrations. 'Evil old woman,' I said, 'the devil has plotted and has sown tares with the wheat so that you will never learn the truth!' " (Duran, 417). Diego Duran displayed a keen interest in the Indian past and indeed composed an extensive chronicle about the Mexica, composed in the 1570s, which numbers among the most important sources on their history. Duran averred that the Indians descended from the Ten Lost Tribes of Israel and that the Toltecs at Tula had been partially evangelized by a Christian apostle, probably St Thomas, whose memory was preserved under the name of Topoltsin-Huemac. The point of these myths was that they explained both the excellence of the native moral code and the similarity of their religious ritual to Christian practice. After a sharp condemnation of those Spaniards who scorned the Indians as more close to beasts than to men, he declared: 'If in their rites and idolatry they displayed blindness and diabolical deceit, at least in the matter of government and politics, in obedience and reverence, in grandeur, they were not surpassed by anyone" (Brading, 124, 283, 284).

THE DEVIL IN PERU

In Peru Fray Vicente de Valverde, the friar who accompanied Pizarro's first expedition to Peru, addressed the Inca Atahualpa, (emperor of the Incan empire) "After establishing this peace and friendship and having submitted willingly or by force, you shall give true obedience to the pope, the supreme pontiff, and receive and believe the faith of Jesus Christ, our God, and scorn and utterly repudiate the abominable superstition of your idols: by this act you shall learn how holy is our law and how false your own, invented by the Devil." (de la Vega, Royal Commentaries, 680) Garcilaso de la Vega (1539-1615) wrote a remarkable work of the origin and development of Indian civilization in Peru, combined with the conquest, be it military or spiritual (Brading, 3).

*

Padre Blas Valera is quoted by de la Vega: Examination of *Comentarios Reales* reveals that Garcilaso repeatedly cited Valera to confirm precisely those aspects of Inca culture, which defined it as an advanced civilization. Brading, 265, 325) There is no doubt that the Devil in his arrogance has always sought to be esteemed and honored as God, not only in the rites and ceremonies of the heathen, but also in some customs of the Christian religion. These customs he had introduced, like an envious monkey, into many regions of the Indians so that he might be the more honored and esteemed by those wretched men. So in one region they practiced oral confession to purge themselves of their sins; in another they washed the heads of children; and elsewhere they kept very rigorous fasts. Sometimes they willingly gave up their lives for their false faith; just as in the Old World faithful Christians offered themselves to martyrdom for the Catholic faith so in the New World the heathen offered themselves to death for the accursed Devil" (Ibid., 82). (Valera was a Peruvian mestizo member of the Company of Jesus, renowned for his knowledge of Quechua and Inca antiquities).

*

Torquemada related a story: "A friar, named Diego de Mercado, a grave man and a dignitary of his Order, one of the most exemplary religious of his time, told and wrote above his signature that years ago he had held a conversation with an Otomi Indian over seventy years old on matters relating to our holy faith. The Indian narrated to him how, long ago, the Otomis were in possession of a book, handed down from father to son and guarded by persons of importance, whose duty it was to explain it. Each page of that book had two columns, and between these columns were paintings which represented Christ crucified, whose features wore the expression of sadness; and such is the God who reigns, they said. For the sake of reverence, they did not turn the leaves with their hands but with a tiny stick kept along with the book for that purpose. The friar having asked the Indian what the contents of the volume were and its teachings the old man could not give the details, but said that, were it in existence yet it would be evident that the teachings of the book and the preaching of the friar were one and the same. But the venerable heirloom had perished in the ground where its guardians had buried it at the arrival of the Spaniards" (De Roo, 424, 425).

*

The conquistador Andres de Tapia, a companion of Cortes, commented: "In this city (Cholula) they had a principal god who at one time had been a man. They called him Quetzalcoatl. He is said to have founded this city, and to have commanded them not to kill men, but instead to build edifices to the creator of the sun and the heavens, in which to offer him quail and other things of the hunt. They were to wish no harm and do no harm to one another. Quetzalcoatl is supposed to have worn a white vesture like a monk's tunic, and over it a mantle covered with red crosses" (*The Conquistadors*, 35).

SAHAGUN ON QUETZALCOATL

According to the Franciscan historian Bernardino Sahagun, Quetzalcoatl was an ancient and revered god throughout Middle America. For this reason his functions and attributes varied considerably in time and space. He was a creator god, a priest, a ruler, a god of learning and science, the planet Venus, the wind. In regard to his influence on the Conquest, we are most concerned with this god as he was understood by the Aztecs" (Dibble, 13).

Before the Aztecs, "Quetzalcoatl was the god of the Toltecs." Sahagun records: "This Quetzalcoatl they considered a god. They all adored him as a god. He was prayed to in olden times there at Tula. . . . And the Toltecs, his vassals, were highly skilled. Nothing that they did was difficult [for them]. They cut green stone, and they cast gold, and they made other works of the craftsman and the feather worker. Very skilled were they. These started and proceeded from Quetzalcoatl—all craft works and wisdom" (Sahagun, 3:13). Unfortunately the theocratic society of which he was the center was replaced by a militaristic society (Dibble, 15).

Bernardino de Sahagun (1499?- 1590) was considered 'the greatest scholar among the Franciscans who mastered Nahuatl, taught in the 1530s and again from the 1570s onwards, and there encountered the native disciples who assisted him in his life-long research into Indian culture. He arrived in New Spain in 1529" (Brading, 119).

"One of the god's names was Ce Acatl Quetzalcoatl (One Reed Quetzalcoatl). The name derives from the date of his birth in the Aztec year One Reed, a recurring year designation. According to the same version, One Reed was also the name of the year of his departure to the east and of his death. The Aztecs assigned their years to the four directions, and the year One Reed was assigned to the east, the direction of abundance, youfulness, light, rebirth, resurrection" (Dibble, 15-16).

The Spaniards also arrived in the year One Reed, 1519; they came in the year and from the direction assigned to Quetzalcoatl (Ibid, 17).

QUETZALCOATL, CREATOR, TEACHER AND LORD. Having a closer look at Quetzalcoatl, to whom was ascribed rites and doctrines similar to those of Christianity we read from Sahagun the words of a confessor to the one who confessed: "Thou wert good, thou wert fine when thou wert sent here, when thy mother, thy father, Quetzalcoatl, made thee, created thee" (Sahagun, 6:31).

Consider again the words of a parent to a daughter concerning the origin of a new life within her: "Perhaps at this time our lord hath instructed thee, hath shown thee mercy? Perhaps for this reason it was determined above us, in the land of the dead, in the beginning, that our lord wisheth to place life within thee? Perhaps it is true that, perchance, the lord, our prince, Quetzalcoatl, the creator, the author, hath permitted it?" (Sahagun, 6:141).

QUETZALCOATL, ONE LORD, ONE GOD

"The men of Yucatan venerated and reverenced this god Quetzalcoatl and they called him Kukulcan" (Landa, 23).

"They adored one lord only whom they believed to be God; they called him Quetzalcoatl and his priest bore the same name and was also called Quetzalcoatl. . . . This priest told them over and over that there was but one god and lord whose name was Quetzalcoatl" (Lafaye, 143).

QUETZALCOATL, AN ALL-POWERFUL DIVINITY

According to Miguel Portilla in *PreColumbian Literatures of Mexico:*

The principal character in the thought of ancient Mexico was Quetzalcoatl. Some times he was considered a god, an all-powerful divinity, and sometimes a culture hero, but he always played an extremely important part in the ancient cultures.

Some Nahuatl myths attribute the origin of present-day human beings, as well as maize, to Quetzalcoatl. As a symbol of divine wisdom, Quetzalcoatl agreed to go to the Region of the Dead and search for the bones of men of other ages. Accompanied only by his nahual, a kind of double or alter ego, Quetzalcoatl descended to the world of the dead. There Mictlantecuhtli, Lord of the Region of the Dead, put him through a series of difficult tests. At last Quetzalcoatl gathered up the bones of a man and a woman and took them to a mythical spot called Tamoanchan. There the gods came together to grind up the bones in a very fine earthen tub, and Quetzalcoatl bled . . . on them to impart life. Here once more blood sacrifice became the source of life and motion. According to the myth, the first humans were called macehuales, which meant the indebted ones; they owed their existence in this fifth age to the sacrifice of Quetzalcoatl.

. . . Along with the myths of Quetzalcoatl in the character of a god, there are others in which he is the great priest of the Toltecs, the culture hero of the pre- Columbian world. His reign is described as a life of abundance with every kind of riches. The

Toltecs received from him wisdom and the arts. Quetzalcoatl, in fasting and chastity, lived in his palaces of different colors which faced toward the four directions of the universe; above all he was devoted to meditation and a search for new ways of understanding divinity.

But this golden age of the Toltecs also came to an end, and Quetzalcoatl had to flee to the east.

. . . Arriving at the edge of the sea on the coast of the Gulf of Mexico, Quetzalcoatl disappeared. According to one version, he embarked on a magic raft of serpents; according to another, he cast himself into a great pyre and emerged as the morning star.

Quetzalcoatl as a culture hero is also found in the ancient Maya texts as Kukulcan and as Gucumatz among the Quiches. All these myths insist that even though Quetzalcoatl went away, he was to return. The god and the priest, often confused in native thinking, continued through the ages as symbol of the most lofty spiritual thought in ancient Mexico" (Portilla, 31-33).

ST. THOMAS AS QUETZALCOATL

For a time Sahagun refused to accept earlier evangelization by St. Thomas or some other missionary: "I have always held that the Gospel had never been preached to them, for I never found anything suggesting Catholic faith, but just the opposite; I found so much idolatry that I refused to believe that the Gospel had been preached to them at any time." Later he wrote: "It seems quite possible that they were evangelized at some time in the past and that after the death of their preachers they completely lost the faith that had been taught them. . . . What inclines me toward this conjecture is the great difficulty I have had in planting the faith among these peoples during the forty years I preached in these regions of Mexico" (Lafaye, 44-145).

Sahagun did not totally exclude an early evangelization of Mexico, but he never suggested that Quetzalcoatl may have been a missionary. He took him for a magician and sorcerer (Ibid., 145).

For Duran and Tovar "the numerous analogies between Quetzalcoatl's conduct, aspect, and speeches and those of an apostle of Christ compel the conclusion that he was a Christian missionary or apostle. . . . Duran and Tovar impressed by the number and quality of their similarities [analogies between Christianity and the ancient Indian religions], refused to reduce them to simple accidental resemblances. This was a natural attitude on the part of Europeans and especially European religious of the sixteenth century, who saw the hidden hand of providence behind all apparent coincidences, a fortiori behind the American realities, regarded as revelations. The theological reasons . . . had convinced them that these analogies were traces of an apostle of Christ, Saint Thomas, the apostle of the Indies" (Ibid., 173-174).

"The idea which soon won out over all others was that Quetzalcoatl was the apostle Saint Thomas, and that all the analogies of belief and ritual between ancient Mexico and Christianity resulted from a very ancient evangelization of America, with a later degradation of Christian doctrine. . . . Another argument, essentially theological, also exerted considerable weight. The Indians seemed innumerable and the New World immense; how could Christ have forgotten a portion of mankind, then believed to be the largest portion of all and to occupy the greatest part of the world [St. John 10:16], in the distribution of mankind he made among his apostles "go and preach to all men?" (St. Matthew 28:19; St. Mark 16:15). Quetzalcoatl alone was well enough known and sufficiently enigmatic to provide a solution to these perplexing questions" (LaFaye, 156-157). In spite of the many analogies the author inserts his opinion, "To our modern way of thinking, [Quetzalcoatl] bears not the slightest resemblance to an apostle of Christ" (Ibid., 157).

Duran suggests the identification of Topiltzin (Quetzalcoatl): "But even though I wish to adhere to the Holy Gospel of Saint Mark, who states that God sent the Holy Apostles to all parts of the world to preach the gospel to His creatures, promising eternal life to baptized believers, I would not dare affirm that Topiltzin was one of the blessed Apostles. Nevertheless, the story of his life has impressed me greatly and has led me and others to believe that, since the natives were also God's creatures, rational and capable of salvation, He cannot have left them without a preacher of the Gospel. And if this is true, that preacher was Topiltzin, who came to this land. According to the story, he was a sculptor who carved admirable images in stone. We read that the glorious apostle Saint Thomas was a master craftsman in the same art. We also know that this apostle was a preacher to the Indians" (Duran, 59).

Appendix I
LDS President John Taylor
on Quetzalcoatl

President John Taylor, prophet and president of The Church of Jesus Christ of Latter-day Saints, 1880-1887, noted in *The Mediation and Atonement* (201), that "the story of the life of the Mexican divinity, Quetzalcoatl, closely resembles that of the Savior; so closely, indeed, that we can come to no other conclusion than that Quetzalcoatl and Christ are the same being." President Taylor quotes from the writings of Lord Kingsborough (1795-1837) as found in his "Antiquities of Mexico." Speaking of a certain plate or painting of the ancient Indians, Kingsborough observed: `Quetzalcoatl is there painted in the attitude of a person crucified, with the impression of nails in his hands and feet, but not actually upon the cross.' Again: `The seventy-third plate of the Borgian MS. is the most remarkable of all, for Quetzalcoatl is not only represented there as crucified upon a cross of Greek form, but his burial and descent into hell are also depicted in a very curious manner.' In another place he observed: 'The Mexicans believe that Quetzalcoatl took human nature upon him, partaking of all the infirmities of man, and was not exempt from sorrow, pain or death, which he suffered voluntarily to atone for the sins of man.'" (Ibid. page 202) Taylor concluded, "When all things are considered, it is almost a wonder that so much of the truth was retained to the days when America became known to Europeans" (Ibid., 203).

Appendix II
Exerpts of the Book of
Mormon that Account
for the Quetzalcoatl Myth

Concerning the prophecy that Jesus (Quetzalcoatl) would come again (according to Mariano Veytia), Montezuma considered Cortes to be a god in the fulfillment of an age old prophecy. It was not long, however, before this false consideration concerning Cortes was realized. The actions of vandalism and thievery of the Spaniards as they invaded the treasuries of Montezuma, looting their gold and other precious items, soon turned Montezuma against Cortes as a god. This raises a question of the original prophecy, would Jesus (Quetzalcoatl) yet return again

The Book of Mormon (a volume of holy scripture comparable to the Bible) includes the story of the visit of Jesus Christ to America after His resurrection in Palestine. It is a record of God's dealings with the ancient inhabitants of the Americas and contains the gospel of Jesus Christ.

The book was written by many ancient prophets by the spirit of prophecy and revelation. Their words, written on gold plates, were quoted and abridged by a prophet-historian named Mormon. The record gives an account of two great civilizations. One came from Jerusalem in 600 BC., and after ward separated into who nations, known as the Nephites and the Lamanites. The other came much earlier when the Lord confounded the tongues at the Tower of Babel. This groups is known as the

Jaredites. After thousands of years, all were destroyed except the Lamanites, and they are the principal ancestors of the American Indians.

The crowning event recorded in the Book of Mormon is the personal ministry of the Lord Jesus Christ among the Nephites soon after his resurrection (in Palestine). It puts forth the doctrines of the gospel, outlines the plan of salvation, and tells men what they must do to gain peace in this life and eternal salvation in the life to come.

After Mormon completed his writings, he delivered the account to his son Moroni, who added a few words of his own and hid up the plates in the hill Cumorah. On September 21, 1823, the same Moroni, then a glorified, resurrected being, appeared to the Prophet Joseph Smith and instructed him relative to the ancient record ad its destined translation into the English language.

In due course the plates were delivered to Joseph Smith, who translated them by the gift and power of God. The record is now published in many languages as a new and additional witness that Jesus Christ is the Son of the living God and that all who will come unto him and obey the laws and ordinances of his gospel may be saved.

THE
BOOK OF MORMON

AN ACCOUNT WRITTEN BY THE HAND OF
MORMON, UPON PLATES TAKEN FROM THE
PLATES OF NEPHI

Wherefore, it is an abridgment of the record the People of Nephi, and also of the Lamanites—written to the Lamanites, which are a remnant of the House of Israel; and also to Jew and Gentile—Written by way of commandment, and also by the spirit of prophesy and of revelation—Written, and sealed up, and hid up unto the Lord, that they might not be destroyed—To come forth by the gift and power of God unto the interpretation thereof—Sealed by the hand of Moroni, and hid up unto the Lord, to come forth in due tine by the way of the Gentile—the interpretation thereof by the gift of God.

An abridgement taken from the Book of Ether also, which is a record of the people of Jared, who were scattered at the time the Lord confounded the language of the people, when they were building a tower to get to heaven—Which is to show unto the remnant of the House of Israel what great things the Lord hath done for their fathers; and that they may know the covenants of the Lord, that they are not cast off forever—And also to the convincing of the Jew and Gentile that JESUS is the CHRIST, the ETERNAL GOD, manifesting himself unto all nations—And now, if there are faults they are the mistakes of men; wherefore, condemn not the things of God, that ye may be found spotless at the judgment-seat of Christ.

BY JOSEPH SMITH, JUNIOR,
AUTHOR AND PROPRIETOR
PRINTED BY E. B. GRANDIN, FOR THE AUTHOR
PALMYRA: 1830.

[*To the reader: It was necessary to list Joseph Smith as author and proprietor in the 1830 edition of the Book Mormon to satisfy copyright laws. In later editions he is listed as translator.*]

The following exerpt of the Book of Mormon begins on page 452 of the First edition (1830). Subsequent editions include division into chapter and verse. The content remains the same.

The previous portion of the Book of Mormon relates the story of a group of people who at 600 B.C. left Jerusalem at the direction of the Lord. They traveled over land and sea, ultimately landing in the promised land [America]. They multiplied, built many cities, divided into two factions, and had many wars and contentions. The more righteous faction was blessed with many prophets and looked forward to the coming of Jesus Christ into the world. This excerpt of the book begins with the signs given them at the time of His birth and continues with the tempest and earthquake, whirlwind and fire at His death, being prior to the personal appearance of Jesus Christ.]

THE ADVENT OF JESUS CHRIST

THE BOOK OF NEPHI

The son of Nephi, which was the son of Helaman.

And Helaman was the son of Helaman, which was the son of Alma, which was the son of Alma, being a descendant of Nephi, which was the son of Lehi, which came out of Jerusalem in the first year of the reign of Zedekiah, the king of Judah.

Now it came to pass that the ninety and first year [of the reign of the judges] had passed away; and it was six hundred years from the time that Lehi left Jerusalem; and it was in the year that Lachoneus was the Chief Judge and the governor over the land. And Nephi the son of Helaman, had departed out of the land of Zarahemla, giving charge unto his son Nephi which was his eldest son concerning the plates of brass, and all the records which had been kept, and all those things which had been kept sacred, from the departure of Lehi out of Jerusalem: then he departed out of the land, and whither he went, no man knoweth; and his son Nephi did keep the records in his stead, yea, the record of this people.

And it came to pass that in the commencement of the ninety and second year, behold, the prophecies of the prophets began to be fulfilled more fully; for there began to be greater signs and greater miracles wrought among the people. But there were some which began to say that the time was past for the words to be fulfilled, which were spoken by Samuel, the

Lamanite. [Samuel had prophesied that in five years from that time the Son of God would be born into the world. The sign was that the night before He came there should be no darkness. "There shall be one day and a night and a day, as if it were one day." Page 445] And they began to rejoice over their brethren, saying, Behold, the time is past, and the words of Samuel are not fulfilled; therefore, your joy and your faith concerning this thing, hath been vain. And it came to pass that they did make a great uproar throughout the land; and the people which believed, began to be very sorrowful, lest by any means those things which had been spoken, might not come to pass. But behold, they did watch steadfastly for that day, and that night, and that day, which shall be as one day, as if there were no night, that they might know that their faith had not been vain.

Now it came to pass that there was a day set apart by the unbelievers, that all those who believed in those traditions, should be put to death, except the sign should come to pass, which had been given by Samuel the prophet. Now it came to pass that when Nephi, the son of Nephi, saw this wickedness of his people, his heart was exceeding sorrowful. And it came to pass that he went out and bowed himself down upon the earth, and cried mightily to his God, in behalf of his people; yea, those which were about to be destroyed because of their faith in the tradition of their fathers. And it came to pass that he cried mightily unto the Lord, all the day; and behold, the voice of the Lord came unto him, saying:

Lift up your head and be of good cheer: for behold, the time is at hand, and on this night shall the sign be given, and on the morrow come I into the world, to shew unto the world that I will fulfill all that which I have caused to be spoken by the mouth of my Holy Prophets. Behold, I come unto my own, to fulfill all things which I have made known unto the children of men, from the foundation of the world, and to do the will, both of the Father, and of the Son of the Father, because of me, and of the Son, because of my flesh. And behold, the time is at hand, and this night shall the sign be given.

And it came to pass that the words which came unto Nephi, were fulfilled, according as they had been spoken: for behold, at the going down of the sun, there was no darkness; and the people began to be astonished, because there was no darkness when the night came. And there were many which had not believed the words of the prophets, fell to the earth, and became as if they were dead, for they knew that the great plan of destruction which they had laid for those who believed in the word of the prophets, had been frustrated; for the sign which had been given was already at hand; and they began to know that the Son of God must shortly appear; yea, in fine, all the people upon the face of the whole earth, from the west to the east, both in the land north and in the land south, were so exceedingly astonished, that they fell to the earth; for they knew that the prophets had testified of these things for many years, and that the sign which had been given, was already at hand; and they began to fear because of their iniquity and their unbelief.

And it came to pass that there was no darkness in all that night, but it was as light as though it was mid-day. And it came to pass that the sun did rise in the morning again, according to its proper order; and they knew that it was the day that the Lord should be born, because of the sign which had been given. And it had come to pass, yea, every whit, according to the words of the prophets. And it came to pass also, that a new star did appear, according to the word.

CATACLYSM

Concerning the tempest and earthquake, whirlwind and fire prior to the personal appearance of Jesus Christ.

And now it came to pass that according to our record, and we know our record to be true, for behold, it was a just man which did keep the record—for he truly did many miracles in the name of Jesus; and there was not any man which could do a miracle in the name of Jesus save he were cleansed every whit from his iniquity—and now it came to pass, if there was no mistake made by this man in the reckoning of our time, the thirty and third year had passed away;[from the signs given of the birth of Jesus Christ into the world] and the people began to look with great earnestness for the sign which had been given by the prophet Samuel, the Lamanite, yea, for the time that there should be darkness for the space of three days, over the face of the land. And there began to be a great doubtings and disputations among the people, notwithstanding so many signs had been given.

And it came to pass in the thirty and fourth year;[Now the Nephites began to reckon their time from this period which the sign was given, or from the coming of Christ. (Page 455)], in the first month, in the fourth day of the month, there arose a great storm, such an one as never had been known in all the land. And there was also a great and terrible tempest; and there was terrible thunder, insomuch that it did shake the whole earth as if it was about to divide asunder. And there were exceeding sharp lightnings, such as never had been known in all the land. And the city of Zarahemla did take fire. And the city of Moroni did sink into the depths of the sea, and the inhabitants thereof were drowned. And the earth was carried up upon the city of Moronihah that in the place of the city there became a great mountain. And there was a great and terrible destruction in the land southward. But behold, there was a more great and terrible destruction in the land northward; for behold, the whole face of the land was changed, because of the tempest and the whirlwinds and the thunderings and the lightnings, and the exceeding great quaking of the whole earth; and the highways were broken up, and the level roads were spoiled, and many smooth places became rough. And many great and notable cities were sunk, and many were burned, and many were shaken till the buildings thereof had fallen to the earth, and the inhabitants thereof were slain, and the places were left desolate. And there were some cities which remained; but the damage thereof was exceeding great, and there were many of them who were slain. And there were some who were carried away in the whirlwind; and whither they went no man knoweth, save they know that they were carried away. And thus the face of the whole earth became deformed, because of the tempests, and the thunderings, and the lightnings, and the quaking of the earth. And behold, the rocks were rent in twain; they were broken up upon the face of the whole earth, insomuch that they were found in broken fragments, and in seams and in cracks, upon all the face of the land.

And it came to pass that when the thunderings, and the lightnings, and the storm, and the tempest, and the quakings of the earth did cease— for behold, they did last for about the space of three hours; and it was said by some that the time was greater; nevertheless, all these great and terrible things were done in about the space of three hours— and then behold, there was darkness upon the face of the land.

And it came to pass that there was thick darkness upon all the face of the land, insomuch that the inhabitants thereof who had not fallen could feel the vapor of darkness; and there could be no light, because of the darkness, neither candles, neither torches; neither could there be fire kindled with their fine and exceedingly dry wood, so that there could not be any light at all; and there was not any light seen, neither fire, nor glimmer, neither the sun, nor the moon, nor the stars, for so great were the mists of darkness which were upon the face of the land.

And it came to pass that it did last for the space of three days that there was no light seen; and there was great mourning and howling and weeping among all the people continually; yea, great were the groanings of the people, because of the darkness and the great destruction which had come upon them. And in one place they were heard to cry, saying: O that we had repented before this great and terrible day, and then would our brethren have been spared, and they would not have been burned in that great city Zarahemla. And in another place they were heard to cry and mourn, saying: O that we had repented before this great and terrible day, and had not killed and stoned the prophets, and cast them out; then would our mothers and our fair daughters, and our children have been spared, and not have been buried up in that great city Moronihah. And thus were the howlings of the people great and terrible.

THE VOICE OF THE LORD IS HEARD

And it came to pass that there was a voice heard among all the inhabitants of the earth, upon all the face of this land, crying: Wo, wo, wo unto this people; wo unto the inhabitants of the whole earth except they shall repent; for the devil laugheth, and his angels rejoice, because of the slain of the fair sons and daughters of my people; and it is because of their iniquity and abominations that they are fallen! Behold, that great city Zarahemla have I burned with fire, and the inhabitants thereof. And behold, that great city Moroni have I caused to be sunk in the depths of the sea, and the inhabitants thereof to be drowned. And behold, that great city Moronihah have I covered with earth, and the inhabitants thereof, to hide their iniquities and their abominations from before my face, that the blood of the prophets and the saints shall not come any more unto me against them. And behold, the city of Gilgal have I caused to be sunk, and the inhabitants thereof to be buried up in the depths of the earth; Yea, and the city of Onihah and the inhabitants thereof, and the city of Mocum and the inhabitants thereof, and the city of Jerusalem and the inhabitants thereof; and waters have I caused to come up in the stead thereof, to hide their wickedness and abominations from before my face, that the blood of the prophets and the saints shall not come up any more unto me against them. And behold, the city of Gadiandi, and the city of Gadiomnah, and the city of Jacob, and the city of Gimgimno, all these have I caused to be sunk, and made hills and valleys in the places thereof; and the inhabitants thereof have I buried up in the depths of the earth, to hide their wickedness and abominations from before my face, that the blood of the prophets and the saints should not come up any more unto me against them. And behold, that great city Jacobugath, which was inhabited by the people of king Jacob, have I caused to be burned with fire because of their sins and their wickedness, which was above all the wickedness of the whole earth, because of their secret murders and combinations; for it was they that did destroy the peace of my people and the government of the land; therefore I did cause them to be burned, to destroy them from before my face, that the blood of the prophets and the saints should not come up unto me any more against them. And behold, the city of Laman, and the city of Josh, and the city of Gad, and the city of Kishkumen, have I caused to be burned with fire, and the inhabitants thereof, because of their wickedness in casting out the prophets, and stoning those whom I did send to declare unto them concerning their wickedness and their abominations. And because they did cast them all out, that there were none righteous among them, I did send down fire and destroy them, that their wickedness and abominations might be hid from before my face, that the blood of the prophets and the saints whom I sent among them might not cry unto me from the ground against them. And many great destructions have I caused to come upon this land, and upon this people, because of their wickedness and their abominations.

O all ye that are spared because ye were more righteous than they, will ye not now return unto me, and repent of your sins, and be converted, that I may heal you? Yea, verily I say unto you, if ye will come unto me ye shall have eternal life. Behold, mine arm of mercy is extended towards you, and whosoever will come, him will I receive; and blessed are those who come unto me. Behold, I am Jesus Christ the Son of God. I created the heavens and the earth, and all things that in them are. I was with the Father from the beginning. I am in the Father, and the Father in me; and in me hath the Father glorified his name. I came unto my own and my own received me not. And the scriptures concerning my coming are fulfilled. And as many as have received me, to them have I given to become the sons of God; and even so will I to as many as shall believe on my name, for behold, by me redemption cometh, and in me is the law of Moses fulfilled. I am the light and the life of the world. I am Alpha and Omega, the beginning and the end. And ye shall offer up unto me no more the shedding of blood; yea, your sacrifices and your burnt offerings shall be done away, for I will accept none of your sacrifices and your burnt offerings. And ye shall offer for a sacrifice unto me a broken heart and a contrite spirit. And whoso cometh unto me with a broken heart and a contrite spirit, him will I baptize with fire and with the Holy Ghost, even as the Lamanites, because of their faith in me at the time of their conversion, were baptized with fire and with the Holy Ghost, and they knew it not. Behold, I have come unto the world to bring redemption unto the world, to save the world from sin. Therefore, whoso repenteth and cometh unto me as a little child, him will I receive, for of such is the kingdom of God. Behold, for such I have laid down my life, and have taken it up again; therefore repent, and come unto me ye ends of the earth, and be saved.

And now behold, it came to pass that all the people of the land did hear these sayings, and did witness of it. And after these sayings there was silence in the land for the space of many hours; for so great was the astonishment of the people that they did cease lamenting and howling for the loss of their kindred which had been slain; therefore there was silence in all the land for the space of many hours.

And it came to pass that there came a voice again unto the people, and all the people did hear, and did witness of it, saying: O ye people of these great cities which have fallen, who are descendants of Jacob, yea, who are of the house of Israel, how oft have I gathered you as a hen gathereth her chickens under her wings, and have nourished you. And again, how oft would I have gathered you as a hen gathereth her chickens under her wings, yea, O ye people of the house of Israel, who have fallen; yea, O ye people of the house of Israel, ye that dwell at

Jerusalem, as ye that have fallen; yea, how oft would I have gathered you as a hen gathereth her chickens, and ye would not. O ye house of Israel whom I have spared, how oft will I gather you as a hen gathereth her chickens under her wings, if ye will repent and return unto me with full purpose of heart. But if not, O house of Israel, the places of your dwellings shall become desolate until the time of the fulfilling of the covenant to your fathers.

And now it came to pass that after the people had heard these words, behold, they began to weep and howl again because of the loss of their kindred and friends. And it came to pass that thus did the three days pass away. And it was in the morning and the darkness dispersed from off the face of the land, and the earth did cease to tremble, and the rocks did cease to rend, and the dreadful groanings did cease, and all the tumultuous noises did pass away. And the earth did cleave together again, that it stood; and the mourning, and the weeping, and the wailing of the people who were spared alive did cease; and their mourning was turned into joy, and their lamentations into the praise and thanksgiving unto the Lord Jesus Christ, their Redeemer. And thus far were the scriptures fulfilled which had been spoken by the prophets. And it was the more righteous part of the people who were saved, and it was they who received the prophets and stoned them not; and it was they who had not shed the blood of the saints, who were spared— and they were spared and were not sunk and buried up in the earth; and they were not drowned in the depths of the sea; and they were not burned by fire, neither were they fallen upon and crushed to death; and they were not carried away in the whirlwind; neither were they overpowered by the vapor of smoke and of darkness. And now, whoso readeth, let him understand; he that hath the scriptures, let him search them, and see and behold if all these deaths and destructions by fire, and by smoke, and by tempests and by whirlwinds, and by the opening of the earth to receive them, and all these things are not unto the fulfilling of the prophecies of many of the holy prophets. Behold, I say unto you, Yea, many have testified of these things at the coming of Christ, and were slain because they testified of these things. Yea, the prophet Zenos did testify of these things, and also Zenock spake concerning these things, because they testified particularly concerning us, who are the remnant of their seed. Behold, our father Jacob also testified concerning a remnant of the seed of Joseph. And behold, are not we a remnant of the seed of Joseph? And these things which testify of us, are they not written upon the plates of brass which our father Lehi brought out of Jerusalem? And it came to pass that in the ending of the thirty and fourth year, behold, I will show unto you that the people of Nephi who were spared, and also those who had been called Lamanites, who had been spared, did have great favors shown unto them, and great blessings poured out upon their heads, insomuch that soon after the ascension of Christ into heaven he did truly manifest himself unto them—showing his body unto them, and ministering unto them; and an account of his ministry shall be given hereafter. Therefore for this time I make an end of my sayings.

APPEARANCE AND TEACHINGS OF JESUS CHRIST
CHAPTER V

Including Introduction of the Son by the Father, doctrine of baptism, prayer, fulfillment of the law of Moses, Blessing little children, Sacrament, Second Coming, Jesus' ascension in the new world, Jesus second coming.

Jesus Christ sheweth himself unto the people of Nephi, as the multitude were gathered together in the land Bountiful, and did minister unto them; and on this wise did he shew himself unto them.

And now it came to pass, that there were a great multitude gathered together, of the people of Nephi, round about the temple which was in the land Bountiful; and they were marveling and wondering one with another, and were showing one to another the great and marvelous change which had taken place. And they were also conversing about this Jesus Christ, of whom the sign had been given concerning his death.

And it came to pass that while they were thus conversing one with another, they heard a voice as if it came out of heaven; and they cast their eyes round about, for they understood not the voice which they heard; and it was not a harsh voice, neither was it a loud voice; nevertheless, and notwithstanding it being a small voice it did pierce them that did hear to the center, insomuch that there was no part of their frame that it did not cause to quake; yea, it did pierce them to the very soul, and did cause their hearts to burn. And it came to pass that again they heard the voice, and they understood it not. And again the third time they did hear the voice, and did open their ears to hear it; and their eyes were towards the sound thereof; and they did look steadfastly towards heaven, from whence the sound came. And behold, the third time they did understand the voice which they heard; and it said unto them: Behold my Beloved Son, in whom I am well pleased, in whom I have glorified my name—hear ye him.

And it came to pass, as they understood they cast their eyes up again towards heaven; and behold, they saw a Man descending out of heaven; and he was clothed in a white robe; and he came down and stood in the midst of them; and the eyes of the whole multitude were turned upon him, and they durst not open their mouths, even one to another, and wist not what it meant, for they thought it was an angel that had appeared unto them.

And it came to pass that he stretched forth his hand and spake unto the people, saying: Behold, I am Jesus Christ, whom the prophets testified shall come into the world. And behold, I am the light and the life of the world; and I have drunk out of that bitter cup which the Father hath given me, and have glorified the Father in taking upon me the sins of the world, in the which I have suffered the will of the Father in all things from the beginning.

And it came to pass that when Jesus had spoken these words the whole multitude fell to the earth; for they remembered that it had been prophesied among them that Christ should show himself unto them after his ascension into heaven.

And it came to pass that the Lord spake unto them saying: Arise and come forth unto me, that ye may thrust your hands into my side, and also that ye may feel the prints of the nails in my hands and in my feet, that ye may know that I am the God of Israel, and the God of the whole earth, and have been slain for the sins of the world.

And it came to pass that the multitude went forth, and thrust their hands into his side, and did feel the prints of the nails in his hands and in his feet; and this they did do, going forth one by one until they had all gone forth, and did see with their eyes and did feel with their hands, and did know of a surety and did bear record, that it was he, of whom it was written by the prophets, that should come.

And when they had all gone forth and had witnessed for themselves, they did cry out with one accord, saying: Hosanna! Blessed be the name of the Most High God! And they did fall down at the feet of Jesus, and did worship him.

And it came to pass that he spake unto Nephi (for Nephi was among the multitude) and he commanded him that he should come forth. And Nephi arose and went forth, and bowed himself before the Lord and did kiss his feet. And the Lord commanded him that he should arise. And he arose and stood before him. And the Lord said unto him: I give unto you power that ye shall baptize this people when I am again ascended into heaven. And again the Lord called others, and said unto them likewise; and he gave unto them power to baptize. And he said unto them: On this wise shall ye baptize; and there shall be no disputations among you. Verily I say unto you, that whoso repenteth of his sins through your words and desireth to be baptized in my name, on this wise shall ye baptize them— Behold, ye shall go down and stand in the water, and in my name shall ye baptize them. And now behold, these are the words which ye shall say, calling them by name, saying: Having authority given me of Jesus Christ, I baptize you in the name of the Father, and of the Son, and of the Holy Ghost. Amen. And then shall ye immerse them in the water, and come forth again out of the water. And after this manner shall ye baptize in my name; for behold, verily I say unto you, that the Father, and the Son, and the Holy Ghost are one ; and I am in the Father, and the Father in me, and the Father and I are one. And according as I have commanded you thus shall ye baptize. And there shall be no disputations among you, as there have hitherto been; neither shall there be disputations among you concerning the points of my doctrine, as there have hitherto been. For verily, verily I say unto you, he that hath the spirit of contention is not of me, but is of the devil, who is the father of contention, and he stirreth up the hearts of men to contend with anger, one with another. Behold, this is not my doctrine, to stir up the hearts of men with anger, one against another; but this is my doctrine, that such things should be done away. Behold, verily, verily, I say unto you, I will declare unto you my doctrine. And this is my doctrine, and it is the doctrine which the Father hath given unto me; and I bear record of the Father, and the Father beareth record of me, and the Holy Ghost beareth record of the Father and me; and I bear record that the Father commandeth all men, everywhere, to repent and believe in me. And whoso believeth in me, and is baptized, the same shall saved; and they are they who shall inherit the kingdom of God. And whoso believeth not in me, and is not baptized, shall be damned. Verily, verily, I say unto you, that this is my doctrine, and I bear record of it from the Father; and whoso believeth in me believeth in the Father also; and unto him will the Father bear record of me, for he will visit him with fire and with the Holy Ghost. And thus will the Father bear record of me, and the Holy Ghost will bear record unto him of the Father and me; for the Father, and I and the Holy Ghost are one. And again I say unto you, ye must repent, and become as a little child, and be baptized in my name, or ye can in nowise receive these things. And again I say unto you, ye must repent, and be baptized in my name, and become as a little child, or ye can in nowise inherit the kingdom of God. Verily, verily, I say unto you, that this is my doctrine, and whoso buildeth upon this buildeth upon my rock, and the gates of hell shall not prevail against them. And whoso shall declare more or less than this, and establish it for my doctrine, the same cometh of evil, and is not built upon my rock; but he buildeth upon a sandy foundation, and the gates of hell stand open to receive such when the floods come and the winds beat upon them. Therefore, go forth unto this people, and declare the words which I have spoken unto the ends of the earth. And it came to pass that when Jesus had spoken these words unto Nephi, and to those who had been called, (now the number of them who had been called, and received power and authority to baptize, was twelve) and behold, he stretched forth his hand unto the multitude, and cried unto them, saying: Blessed are ye if ye shall give heed unto the words of these twelve whom I have chosen from among you to minister unto you, and to be your servants; and unto them I have given power that they may baptize you with water; and after that ye are baptized with water, behold, I will baptize you with fire and with the Holy Ghost; therefore blessed are ye if ye shall believe in me and be baptized, after that ye have seen me and know that I am. And again, more blessed are they who shall believe in your words because that ye shall testify that ye have seen me, and that ye know that I am. Yea, blessed are they who shall believe in your words, and come down into the depths of humility and be baptized, for they shall be visited with fire and with the Holy Ghost, and shall receive a remission of their sins. Yea, blessed are the poor in spirit who come unto me, for theirs is the kingdom of heaven. And again, blessed are all they that mourn, for they shall be comforted. And blessed are the meek, for they shall inherit the earth. And blessed are all they who do hunger and thirst after righteousness, for they shall be filled with the Holy Ghost. And blessed are the merciful, for they shall obtain mercy. And blessed are all the pure in heart, for they shall see God. And blessed are all the peacemakers, for they shall be called the children of God. And blessed are all they who are persecuted for my name's sake, for theirs is the kingdom of heaven. And blessed are ye when men shall revile you and persecute, and shall say all manner of evil against you falsely, for my sake; for ye shall have great joy and be exceeding glad, for great shall be your reward in heaven; for so persecuted they the prophets who were before you. Verily, verily, I say unto you, I give unto you to be the salt of the earth; but if the salt shall lose its savor wherewith shall the earth be salted? The salt shall be thenceforth good for nothing, but to be cast out and to be trodden under foot of men. Verily, verily, I say unto you, I give unto you to be the light of this people. A city that is set on a hill cannot be hid. Behold, do men light a candle and put it under a bushel? Nay, but on a candlestick, and it giveth light to all that are in the house; therefore let your light so shine before this people, that they may see your good works and glorify your Father who is in heaven. Think not that I am come to destroy the law or the prophets. I am not come to destroy but to fulfil; For verily I say unto you, one jot nor one tittle hath not passed away from the law, but in me it hath all been fulfilled.

And behold, I have given you the law and the commandments of my Father, that ye shall believe in me, and that ye shall repent of your sins, and come unto me with a broken heart and a contrite spirit. Behold, ye have the commandments before you, and the law is fulfilled. Therefore come unto me and be ye saved; for verily I say unto you, that except ye shall keep my commandments, which I have commanded you at this time, ye shall in no case enter into the kingdom of heaven. Ye have heard that it hath been said by them of old time, and it is also written before you, that thou shalt not kill, and whosoever shall kill shall be in danger of the judgment of God ; but I say unto you, that whosoever is angry with his brother shall be in danger of his judgment. And whosoever shall say to his brother, Raca, shall be in danger of the council; and whosoever shall say, Thou fool, shall be in danger of hell fire. Therefore, if ye shall come unto me, or shall desire to come unto me, and rememberest that thy brother hath aught against thee—go thy way unto thy brother, and first be reconciled to thy brother, and then come unto me with full purpose of heart, and I will receive you. Agree with thine adversary quickly while thou art in the way with him, lest at any time he shall get thee, and thou shalt be cast into prison. Verily, verily, I say unto thee, thou shalt by no means come out thence until thou hast paid the uttermost senine. And while ye are in prison can ye pay even one senine? Verily, verily, I say unto you, Nay. Behold, it is written by them of old time, that thou shalt not commit adultery; but I say unto you, that whosoever looketh on a woman, to lust after her, hath committed adultery already in his heart. Behold, I give unto you a commandment, that ye suffer none of these things to enter into your heart; for it is better that ye should deny yourselves of these things, wherein ye will take up your cross, than that ye should be cast into hell. It hath been written, that whosoever shall put away his wife, let him give her a writing of divorcement. Verily, verily, I say unto you, that whosoever shall put away his wife, saving for the cause of fornication, causeth her to commit adultery; and whoso shall marry her who is divorced committeth adultery. And again it is written, thou shalt not forswear thyself, but shalt perform unto the Lord thine oaths; but verily, verily, I say unto you, swear not at all; neither by heaven, for it is God's throne; nor by the earth, for it is his footstool; neither shalt thou swear by the head, because thou canst not make one hair black or white; but let your communication be Yea, yea; Nay, nay; for whatsoever cometh of more than these is evil. And behold, it is written, an eye for an eye, and a tooth for a tooth; but I say unto you, that ye shall not resist evil, but whosoever shall smite thee on thy right cheek, turn to him the other also; and if any man will sue thee at the law and take away thy coat, let him have thy cloak also; and whosoever shall compel thee to go a mile, go with him twain. Give to him that asketh thee, and from him that would borrow of thee turn thou not away. And behold it is written also, that thou shalt love thy neighbor and hate thine enemy; but behold I say unto you, love your enemies, bless them that curse you, do good to them that hate you, and pray for them who despitefully use you and, persecute you; that ye may be the children of your Father who is in heaven; for he maketh his sun to rise on the evil and on the good. Therefore those things which were of old time, which were under the law, in me are all fulfilled. Old things are done away, and all things have become new. Therefore I would that ye should be perfect even as I, or your Father who is in heaven is perfect. Verily, verily, I say that I would that ye should do alms unto the poor; but take heed; that ye do not your alms before men to be seen of them; otherwise ye have no reward of your Father who is in heaven. Therefore, when ye shall do your alms do not sound a trumpet before you, as will hypocrites do in the synagogues and in the streets, that they may have glory of men. Verily I say unto you, they have their reward. But when thou doest alms let not thy left hand know what thy right hand doeth; that thine alms may be in secret; and thy Father who seeth in secret, himself shall reward thee openly.

And when thou prayest thou shalt not do as the hypocrites, for they love to pray, standing in the synagogues and in the comers of the streets, that they may be seen of men. Verily I say unto you, they have their reward. But thou, when thou prayest, enter into thy closet, and when thou hast shut thy door, pray to thy Father who is in secret; and thy Father, who seeth in secret, shall reward thee openly. But when ye pray use not vain repetitions, as the heathen, for they think that they shall be heard for their much speaking. Be not ye therefore like unto them, for your Father knoweth what things ye have need of before ye ask him. After this manner therefore pray ye: Our Father who art in heaven, hallowed be they name. Thy will be done on earth as it is in heaven. And forgive us our debts, as we forgive our debtors. And lead us not into temptation, but deliver us from evil. For thine is the kingdom, and the power, and the glory, for-ever. Amen. For, if ye forgive men their trespasses your heavenly Father will also forgive you; but if ye forgive not men their trespasses neither will your Father forgive your trespasses. Moreover, when ye fast be not as the hypocrites, of a sad countenance, for they disfigure their faces that they may appear unto men to fast. Verily I say unto you, they have their reward. But thou, when thou fastest, anoint thy head, and wash thy face; that thou appear not unto men to fast, but unto thy Father, who is in secret; and thy Father, who seeth in secret, shall reward thee openly.

Lay not up for yourselves treasures upon earth, where moth and rust doth corrupt, and thieves break through and steal; but lay up for yourselves treasures in heaven, where neither moth nor rust doth corrupt, and where thieves do not break through nor steal. For where your treasure is, there will your heart be also. The light of the body is the eye; if, therefore, thine eye be single, thy whole body shall be full of light. But if thine eye be evil, thy whole body shall be full of darkness. If, therefore, the light that is in thee be darkness, how great is that darkness! No man can serve two masters; for either he will hate the one and love the other, or else he will hold to the one and despise the other. Ye cannot serve God and Mammon.

CHAPTER VI

And now it came to pass that when Jesus had spoken these words, he looked upon the twelve whom he had chosen, and said unto them: Remember the words which I have spoken. For behold, ye are they whom I have chosen to minister unto this people. Therefore I say unto you, take no thought for your life, what ye shall eat, or what ye shall drink; nor yet for your body, what ye shall put on. Is not the life more than meat, and the body than raiment? Behold the fowls of the air, for they sow not, neither do they reap nor gather into barns: yet your heavenly Father feedeth them. Are ye not much better than they? Which of you by taking thought can add one cubit unto his stature? And why take ye thought for raiment? Consider the lilies of the field how they grow; they toil not, neither do they spin; and yet I say unto you, that even Solomon, in all his glory, was not arrayed like one of these. Wherefore, if God so clothe the grass of the field, which today is, and tomorrow is cast into the oven, even so will he clothe you, if ye are not of little faith. Therefore take no thought, saying, What shall we eat? or, What shall we drink? or, Wherewithal shall we be clothed? For your heavenly Father knoweth that ye have need of all these things. But seek ye first the kingdom of God and his righteousness, and all these things shalt be added unto you. Take therefore no thought for the morrow, for the morrow shall take thought for the things of itself. Sufficient is the day unto the evil thereof.

And now it came to pass that when Jesus had spoken these word, he turned again to the multitude, and did open his mouth unto them again, saying: Verily, verily, I say unto you, judge not, that ye be not judged. For with what judgment ye judge, ye shall be judged; and with what measure ye mete, it I shall be measured to you again. And why beholdest thou the mote that is in thy brother's eye, but considerest not the beam that is in thine own eye? Or how wilt thou say to thy brother: Let me pull the mote out of thine eye—and behold, a beam is in thine own eye? Thou hypocrite, first cast the beam out of thine own eye; and then shalt thou see clearly to cast the mote out of thy brother's eye. Give not that which is holy unto the dogs, neither cast ye your pearls before swine, lest they trample them under their feet, and turn again and rend you.

Ask, and it shall be given unto you; seek, and ye shall find; knock, and it shall be opened unto you. For everyone that asketh, receiveth; and he that seeketh, findeth; and to him that knocketh, it shall be opened. Or what man is there of you, who, if his son ask bread, will give him a stone? Or if he ask a fish, will he give him a serpent? If ye then, being evil, know how to give good gifts unto your children, how much more shall your Father who is in heaven give good things to them that ask him? Therefore, all things whatsoever ye would that men should do to you, do ye even so to them, for this is the law and the prophets. Enter ye in at the strait gate; for wide is the gate, and broad is the way, which leadeth to destruction, and many there be who go in thereat; because strait is the gate, and narrow is the way, which leadeth unto life, and few there be that find it. Beware of false prophets who come to you in sheep's clothing, but inwardly they are ravening wolves. Ye shall know them by their fruits. Do men gather grapes of thorns, or figs of thistles? Even so every good tree bringeth forth good fruit; but a corrupt tree bringeth forth evil fruit. A good tree cannot bring forth evil fruit, neither a corrupt tree bring forth good fruit. Every tree that bringeth not forth good fruit is hewn down, and cast into the fire. Wherefore, by their fruits ye shall know them. Not every one that saith unto me, Lord, Lord, shall enter into the kingdom of heaven; but he that doeth the will of my Father who is in heaven. Many will say to me in that day: Lord, Lord, have we not prophesied in thy name, and in thy name have cast out devils, and in thy name done many wonderful works? And then will I profess unto them: I never knew you; depart from me, ye that work iniquity. Therefore, whoso heareth these sayings of mine and doeth them, I will liken him unto a wise man, who built his house upon a rock—and the rain descended, and the floods came, and the winds blew, and beat upon that house; and it fell not, for it was founded upon a rock. And every one that heareth these sayings of mine and doeth them not shall be likened unto a foolish man, who built his house upon the sand. And the rain descended, and the floods came, and the winds blew, and beat upon that house; and it fell, and great was; the fall of it.

CHAPTER VII

And now it came to pass that when Jesus had ended these sayings he cast his eyes round about on the multitude, and said unto them: Behold, ye have heard the things which I taught before I ascended to my Father; therefore, whoso remembereth these sayings of mine and doeth them, him will I raise up at the last day. And it came to pass that when Jesus had said these words, he perceived that there were some among them who marveled, and wondered what he would concerning the law of Moses; for they understood not the saying that old things had passed away, and that all things had become new. And he said unto them: Marvel not that I said unto you that old things had passed away, and that all things had become new. Behold, I say unto you that the law is fulfilled that was given unto Moses. Behold, I am he who gave the law, and I am he who covenanted with my people Israel; therefore, the law in me is fulfilled, for I have come to fulfil the law; therefore it hath an end. Behold, I do not destroy the prophets, for as many as have not been fulfilled in me, verily I say unto you, shall all be fulfilled. And because I said unto you that old things have passed away, I do not destroy that which hath been spoken concerning things which are to come. For behold, the covenant which I have made with my people is not all fulfilled; but the law which was given unto Moses hath an end in me. Behold. I am the law, and the light. Look unto me, and endure to the end, and ye shall live; for unto him that endureth to the end will I give eternal life. Behold, I have given unto you the commandments; therefore keep my commandments. And this is the law and the prophets, for they truly testified of me.

And now it came to pass that when Jesus had spoken these words, he said unto those twelve whom he had chosen: Ye are my disciples; and ye are a light unto this people, who are a remnant of the house of Joseph. And behold, this is the land of your inheritance; and the Father hath given it unto you. And not at any time hath the Father given me commandment that I should tell it unto your brethren at Jerusalem. Neither at any time hath the Father given me commandment that I should tell unto them concerning the other tribes of the house of Israel, whom the Father hath led away out of the land. This much did the Father command me, that I should tell unto them: That other sheep I have which are not of this fold; them also I must bring, and they shall hear my voice; and there shall be one fold, and one shepherd. And now, because of stiffneckedness and unbelief they understood not my word; therefore I was commanded to say no more of the Father concerning this thing unto them. But, verily, I say unto you that the Father hath commanded me, and I tell it unto you, that ye were separated from among them because of their iniquity; therefore it is because of their iniquity that they know not of you. And verily, I say unto you again that the other tribes hath the Father separated from them; and it is because of their iniquity that they know not of them. And verily I say unto you, that ye are they of whom I said: Other sheep I have which are not of this fold; them also I must bring, and they shall hear my voice; and there shall be one fold, and one shepherd. And they understood me not, for they supposed it had been the Gentiles; for they understood not that the Gentiles should be converted through their preaching. And they understood me not that I said they shall hear my voice; and they understood me not that the Gentiles should not at any time hear my voice—that I should not manifest myself unto them save it were by the Holy Ghost. But behold, ye have both heard my voice, and seen me; and ye are my sheep, and ye are numbered among those whom the Father hath given me. And verily, verily, I say unto you that I have other sheep which are not of this land, neither of the land of Jerusalem, neither in any parts of that land round about whither I have been to minister. For they of whom I speak are they who have not as yet heard my voice; neither have I at any time manifested myself unto them. But I have received a commandment of the Father that I shall go unto them, and that they shall hear my voice, and shall be numbered among my sheep that there may be one fold and one shepherd; therefore I go to show myself unto them. And I command you that ye shall write these sayings after I am gone, that if it so be that my people at Jerusalem, they who have seen me and been with me in my ministry, do not ask the Father in my name, that they may receive a knowledge of you by the Holy Ghost, and also of the other tribes whom they know not of, that these sayings which ye shall write shall be kept and shall be manifested unto the Gentiles, that through the fulness of the

Gentiles, the remnant of their seed, who shall be scattered forth upon the face of the earth because of their unbelief, may be brought in, or may be brought to a knowledge of me, their Redeemer. And then will I gather them in from the four quarters of the earth; and then will I fulfill the covenant which the Father hath made unto all the people of the house of Israel. And blessed are the Gentiles, because of their belief in me, in and of the Holy Ghost, which witnesses unto them of me and of the Father. Behold, because of their belief in me, saith the Father, and because of the unbelief of you, O house of Israel, in the latter day shall the truth come unto the Gentiles, that the fulness of these things shall be made known unto them. But wo, saith the Father, unto the unbelieving of the Gentiles—for notwithstanding they have come forth upon the face of this land, and have scattered my people who are of the house of Israel; and my people who are of the house of Israel have been cast out from among them, and have been trodden under feet by them; and because of the mercies of the Father unto the Gentiles, and also the judgments of the Father upon my people who are of the house of Israel, verily, verily, I say unto you, that after all this, and I have caused my people who are of the house of Israel to be smitten, and to be afflicted, and to be slain, and to be cast out from among them, and to become hated by them, and to become a hiss and a byword among them—and thus commandeth the Father that I should say unto you: At that day when the Gentiles shall sin against my gospel, and shall be lifted up in the pride of their hearts above all nations, and above all the people of the whole earth, and shall be filled with all manner of lyings, and of deceits, and of mischiefs, and all manner of hypocrisy, and murders, and priestcrafts, and whoredoms, and of secret abominations; and if they shall do all those things, and shall reject the fulness of my gospel, behold, saith the Father, I will bring the fulness of my gospel from among them. And then will I remember my covenant which I have made unto my people, O house of Israel, and I will bring my gospel unto them. And I will show unto thee, O house of Israel, that the Gentiles shall not have power over you; but I will remember my covenant unto you, O house of Israel, and ye shall come unto the knowledge of the fulness of my gospel. But if the Gentiles will repent and return unto me, saith the Father, behold they shall be numbered among my people, O house of Israel. And I will not suffer my people, who are of the house of Israel, to go through among them, and tread them down, saith the Father. But if they will not turn unto me, and hearken unto my voice, I will suffer them, yea, I will suffer my people, O house of Israel, that they shall go through among them, and shall tread them down, and they shall be as salt that hath lost its savor, which is thenceforth good for nothing but to be cast out, and to be trodden under foot of my people, O house of Israel. Verily, verily, I say unto you, thus hath the Father commanded me—that I should give unto this people this land for their inheritance. And then the words of the prophet Isaiah shall be fulfilled, which say: Thy watchmen shall lift up the voice; with the voice together shall they sing, for they shall see eye to eye when the Lord shall bring again Zion. Break forth into joy, sing together, ye waste places of Jerusalem; for the Lord hath comforted his people, he hath redeemed Jerusalem. The Lord hath made bare his holy arm in the eye of all the nations; and all the ends of the earth shall see the salvation of God.

CHAPTER VIII

Behold, now it came to pass that when Jesus had spoken these words he looked round about again on the multitude, and he said unto them: Behold, my time is at hand. I perceive that ye are weak, that ye cannot understand all my words which I am commanded of the Father to speak unto you at this time. Therefore, go ye unto your homes, and ponder upon the things which I have said, and ask of the Father, in my name, that ye may understand, and prepare your minds for the morrow, and I come unto you again. But now I go unto the Father, and also to show myself unto the lost tribes of Israel, for they are not lost unto the Father, for he knoweth whither he hath taken them.

And it came to pass that when Jesus had thus spoken, he cast his eyes round about again on the multitude, and beheld they were in tears, and did look steadfastly upon him as if they would ask him to tarry a little longer with them. And he said unto them: Behold, my bowels are filled with compassion towards you. Have ye any that are sick among you? Bring them hither. Have ye any that are lame, or blind, or halt, or maimed, or leprous, or that are withered, or that are deaf, or that are afflicted in any manner? Bring them hither and I will heal them, for I have compassion upon you; my bowels are filled with mercy. For I perceive that ye desire that I should show unto you what I have done unto your brethren at Jerusalem, for I see that your faith is sufficient that I should heal you.

And it came to pass that when he had thus spoken, all the multitude, with one accord, did go forth with their sick and their afflicted, and their lame, and with their blind, and with their dumb, and with all them that were afflicted in any manner; and he did heal them everyone as they were brought forth unto him. And they did all, both they who had been healed and they who were whole, bow down at his feet, and did worship him; and as many as could come for the multitude did worship him; and as many as could come for the multitude did kiss his feet, insomuch that they did bathe his feet with their tears.

And it came to pass that he commanded that their little children should be brought. So they brought their little children and set them down upon the ground round about him, and Jesus stood in the midst; and the multitude gave way till they had all been brought unto him. And it came to pass that when they had all been brought, and Jesus stood in the midst, he commanded the multitude that they should kneel down upon the ground. And it came to pass that when they had knelt upon the ground, Jesus groaned within himself, and said: Father, I am troubled because of the wickedness of the people of the house of Israel. And when he had said these words, he himself also knelt upon the earth; and behold he prayed unto the Father, and the things which he prayed cannot be written, and the multitude did bear record who heard him. And after this manner do they bear record: The eye hath never seen, neither hath the ear heard, before, so great and marvelous things as we saw and heard Jesus speak unto the Father; and no tongue can speak, neither can there be written by any man, neither can the hearts of men conceive so great and marvelous things as we both saw and heard Jesus speak; and no one can conceive of the joy which filled our souls at the time we heard him pray for us unto the Father.

And it came to pass that when Jesus had made an end of praying unto the Father, he arose; but so great was the joy of the multitude that they were overcome. And it came to pass that Jesus spake unto them, and bade them arise. And they arose from the earth, and he said unto them: Blessed are ye because of your faith. And now behold, my joy is full. And when he had said these words, he wept, and the multitude bare record of it, and he took their little children, one by one, and blessed them and prayed unto the Father for them. And when he had done this he wept again; and he spake unto the multitude, and said unto them: Behold your little ones. And as they looked to behold they cast their eyes towards heaven, and they saw the heavens open, and they saw angels descending out of heaven as it were in the midst of fire; and they came down and encircled those little ones about, and they were encircled about with fire; and the angels did minister unto them. And the multitude did see and hear and bear record; and they know that their record is true for they all of them did see and hear, every man for himself; and they were in number about two thousand and five hundred souls; and they did consist of men, women, and children.

And it came to pass that Jesus commanded his disciples that they should bring forth some bread and wine unto him. And while they were gone for bread and wine, he commanded the multitude that they should sit themselves down upon the earth.

And when the disciples had come with bread and wine, he took of the bread and brake and blessed it; and he gave unto the disciples and commanded that they should eat. And when they had eaten and were filled, he commanded that they should give unto the multitude. And when the multitude had eaten and were filled, he said unto the disciples: Behold there shall one be ordained among you, and to him will I give power that he shall break bread and bless it and give it unto the people of my church, unto all those who shall believe and be baptized in my name. And this shall ye always observe to do, even as I have done, even as I have broken bread and blessed it and given it unto you. And this shall ye do in remembrance of my body, which I have shown unto you. And it shall be a testimony unto the Father that ye do always remember me. And if ye do always remember me ye shall have my Spirit to be with you.

And it came to pass that when he said these words, he commanded his disciples that they should take of the wine of the cup and drink of it, and that they should also give unto the multitude that they might drink of it. And it came to pass. that they did so, and did drink of it and were filled; and they gave unto the multitude, and they did drink, and they were filled. And when the disciples had done this, Jesus said unto them: Blessed are ye for this thing which ye have done, for this is fulfilling my commandments, and this doth witness unto the Father that ye are willing to do that which I have commanded you. And this shall ye always do to those who repent and are baptized in my name; and ye shall do it in remembrance of my blood, which I have shed for you, that ye may witness unto the Father that ye do always remember me. And if ye do always remember me ye shall have my Spirit to be with you. And I give unto you a commandment that ye shall do these things. And if ye shall always do these things blessed are ye, for ye are built upon my rock. But whoso among you shall do more or less than these are not built upon my rock, but are built upon a sandy foundation; and when the rain descends, and the floods come, and the winds blow, and beat upon them, they shall fall, and the gates of hell are ready open to receive them. Therefore blessed are ye if ye shall keep my commandments, which the Father hath commanded me that I should give unto you. Verily, verily, I say unto you, ye must watch and pray always, lest ye be tempted by the devil, and ye be led away captive by him. And as I have prayed among you even so shall ye pray in my church, among my people who do repent and are baptized in my name. Behold I am the light; I have set an example for you.

And it came to pass that when Jesus had spoken these words unto his disciples, he turned again unto the multitude and said unto them: Behold, verily, verily, I say unto you, ye must watch and pray always lest ye enter into temptation; for Satan desireth to have you, that he may sift you as wheat. Therefore ye must always pray unto the Father in my name; and whatsoever ye shall ask the Father in my name, which is right, believing that ye shall receive behold it shall be given unto you. Pray in your families unto the Father, always in my name, that your wives and your children may be blessed. And behold, ye shall meet together oft; and ye shall not forbid any man from coming unto you when ye shall meet together, but suffer them that they may come unto you and forbid them not; but ye shall pray for them, and shall not cast them out; and if it so be that they come unto you oft ye shall pray for them unto the Father, in my name. Therefore, hold up your light that it may shine unto the world. Behold I am the light which ye shall hold up—that which ye have seen me do. Behold ye see that I have prayed unto the Father, and ye all have witnessed. And ye see that I have commanded that none of you should go away, but rather have commanded that ye should come unto me, that ye might feel and see; even so shall ye do unto the world; and whosoever breaketh this commandment suffereth himself to be led into temptation.

And now it came to pass that when Jesus had spoken these words, he turned his eyes again upon the disciples whom he had chosen, and said unto them: Behold verily, verily, I say unto you, I give unto you another commandment, and then I must go unto my Father that I may fulfil other commandments which he hath given me. And now behold, this is the commandment which I give unto you, that ye shall not suffer any one knowingly to partake of my flesh and blood unworthily, when ye shall minister it; for whoso eateth and drinketh my flesh and blood unworthily eateth and drinketh damnation to his soul; therefore if ye know that a man is unworthy to eat and drink of my flesh and blood ye shall forbid him. Nevertheless, ye shall not cast him out from among you, but ye shall minister unto him and shall pray for him unto the Father, in my name; and if it so be that he repenteth and is baptized in my name, then shall ye receive him, and shall minister unto him of my flesh and blood. But if he repent not he shall not be numbered among my people, that he may not destroy my people, for behold I know my sheep, and they are numbered. Nevertheless, ye shall not cast him out of your synagogues, or your places of worship, for unto such shall ye continue to minister; for ye know not but what that they will return and repent, and come unto me with full purpose of heart, and I shall heal them; and ye shall be the means of bringing salvation unto them. Therefore, keep these sayings which I have commanded you that ye come not under condemnation; for wo unto him whom the Father condemneth. And I give you these commandments because of the disputations which have been among you. And blessed are ye if ye have no disputations among you. And now I go unto the Father, because it is expedient that I should go unto the Father for your sakes.

And it came to pass that when Jesus had made an end of these sayings, he touched with his hand the disciples whom he had chosen, one by one, even until he had touched them all, and spake unto them as he touched them. And the multitude heard not the words which he spake, therefore they did not bear record; but the disciples bare record that he gave them power to give the Holy Ghost. And I will show unto you hereafter that this record is true.

And it came to pass that when Jesus had touched them all, there came a cloud and overshadowed the multitude that they could not see Jesus. And while they were overshadowed he departed from them, and ascended into heaven. And the disciples saw and did bear record that he ascended again into heaven.

CHAPTER IX

And now it came to pass that when Jesus had ascended into heaven, the multitude did disperse, and every man did take his wife and his children and did return to his own home. And it was noised abroad among the people immediately, before it was yet dark, that the multitude had seen Jesus, and that he had ministered unto them, and that he would also show himself on the morrow unto the multitude. Yea, and even all the night it was noised abroad concerning Jesus; and insomuch did they send forth unto the people that there were many, yea, an exceeding great number, did labor exceedingly all that night, that they might be on the morrow in the place where Jesus should show him unto the multitude.

And it came to pass that on the morrow, when the multitude was gathered together, behold, Nephi and his brother whom he had raised from the dead, whose name was Timothy, and also his son, whose name was Jonas, and also Mathoni, and Mathonihah, his brother, and Kumen, and Kumenonhi, and Jeremiah, and Shemnon, and Jonas, and Zedekiah, and Isaiah—now these were the names of the disciples whom Jesus had chosen—and it came to pass that they went forth and stood in the midst of the multitude. And behold, the multitude was so great that they did cause that they should be separated into twelve bodies. And the twelve did teach the multitude; and behold, they did cause that the multitude should kneel down upon the face of the earth, and should pray unto the Father in the name of Jesus. And the disciples did pray unto the Father also in the name of Jesus. And it came to pass that they arose and ministered unto the people. And when they had ministered those same words which Jesus had spoken nothing varying from the words which Jesus had spoken— behold, they knelt again and prayed to the Father in the name of Jesus. And they did pray for that which they most desired; and they desired that the Holy Ghost should be given unto them. And when they had thus prayed they went down unto the water's edge, and the multitude followed them. And it came to pass that Nephi went down into the water and was baptized. And he came up out of the water and began to baptize. And he baptized all those whom Jesus had chosen. And it came to pass when they were all baptized and had come up out of the water, the Holy Ghost did fall upon them, and they were filled with the Holy Ghost and with fire. And behold, they were encircled about as if it were by fire; and it came down from heaven, and the multitude did witness it, and did bear record; and angels did come down out of heaven and did minister unto them. And it came to pass that while the angels were ministering unto the disciples, behold, Jesus came and stood in the midst and ministered unto them. And it came to pass that he spake unto the multitude, and commanded them that they should kneel down again upon the earth, and also that his disciples should kneel down upon the earth. And it came to pass that when they had all knelt down upon the earth, he commanded his disciples that they should pray. And behold, they began to pray; and they did pray unto Jesus, calling him their Lord and their God.

And it came to pass that, Jesus departed out of the midst of them, and went a little way off from them and bowed himself to the earth, and he said: Father, I thank thee that thou hast given the Holy Ghost unto these whom I have chosen; and it is because of their belief in me that I have chosen them out of the world. Father, I pray thee that thou wilt give the Holy Ghost unto all them that shall believe in their words. Father, thou hast given them the Holy Ghost because they believe in me; and thou seest that they believe in me because thou hearest them, and they pray unto me; and they pray unto me because I am with them. And now Father, I pray unto thee for them, and also for all those who shall believe on their words, that they may believe in me, that I may be in them as thou, Father, art in me, that we may be one.

And it came to pass that when Jesus had thus prayed unto the Father, he came unto his disciples, and behold, they did still continue, without ceasing, to pray unto him; and they did not multiply many words, for it was given unto them what they should pray, and they were filled with desire. And it came to pass that Jesus blessed them as they did pray unto him; and his countenance did smile upon them, and the light of his countenance did shine upon them, and behold they were as white as the countenance and also the garments of Jesus; and behold the whiteness thereof did exceed all the whiteness thereof, yea, even there could be nothing upon earth so white as the whiteness thereof. And Jesus said unto them: Pray on; nevertheless they did not cease to pray. And he turned from them again, and went a little way off and bowed himself to the earth; and he prayed again unto the Father, saying: Father, I thank thee that thou hast purified those whom I have chosen, because of their faith, and I pray for them, and also for them who shall believe on their words, that they may be purified in me, through faith on their words, even as they are purified in me. Father, I pray not for the world, but for those whom thou hast given me out of the world, because of their faith, that they may be purified in me, that I may be in them as thou, Father, art in me, that we may be one, that I may be glorified in them.

And it came to pass that when Jesus had spoken these words he came again unto his disciples; and behold they did pray steadfastly, without ceasing, unto him; and he did smile upon them again; and behold they were white even as Jesus.

And it came to pass that he went again a little way off and prayed unto the Father; and tongue cannot speak the words which he prayed, neither can be written by man the words which he prayed. And the multitude did hear and do bear record; and their hearts were open and they did understand in their hearts the words which he prayed. Nevertheless, so great and marvelous were the words which he prayed that they cannot be written, neither can they be uttered by man.

And it came to pass that when Jesus had made an end of praying he came again to the disciples, and said unto them: So great faith have I never seen among all the Jews; wherefore I could not show unto them so great miracles, because of their unbelief. Verily I say unto you, there are none of them that have seen so great things as ye have seen; neither have they heard so great things as ye have heard.

And it came to pass that he commanded the multitude that they should cease to pray, and also his disciples. And he commanded them that they should not cease to pray in their hearts. And he commanded them that they should arise and stand up upon their feet. And they arose up and stood upon their feet. And it came to pass that he brake bread again and blessed it, and gave to the disciples to eat. And when they had eaten he commanded them that they should break bread, and give unto the multitude. And when they had given unto the multitude he also gave them wine to drink, and commanded them that they should give unto the multitude. Now, there had been no bread, neither wine, brought by the disciples, neither by the multitude; but he truly gave unto them bread to eat, and also wine to drink. And he said unto them: He that eateth this bread eateth of my body to his soul; and he that drinketh of this wine drinketh of my blood to his soul; and his soul shall never hunger or thirst, but shall be filled. Now, when the multitude had all eaten and drunk, behold, they were filled with the Spirit; and they did cry out with one voice, and gave glory to Jesus, whom they both saw and heard. And it came to pass that when they had all given glory unto Jesus, he said unto them: Behold now I finish the commandment which the Father hath commanded me concerning this people, who are a remnant of the house of Israel. Ye remember that I spake unto you, and said that when the words of Isaiah should be fulfilled—behold they are written, ye have them before you, therefore search them—and verily, verily, I say unto you, that when they shall be fulfilled then is the fulfilling of the covenant which the Father hath made unto his people; O house of Israel. And then shall the remnants which shall be scattered abroad upon the face of the earth, be gathered in from the east and from the west, and from the south and from the north; and they shall be brought to the knowledge of the Lord their God, who hath redeemed them. And the Father hath commanded me that I should give unto you this land, for your inheritance. And I say unto you, that if the Gentiles do not repent after the blessing which they shall receive, after they have scattered my people—then shall ye, who are a remnant of the house of Jacob, go forth among them; and ye shall be in the midst of them who shall be many; and ye shall be among them as a lion among the beasts of the forest, and as a young lion among the flocks of sheep, who, if he goeth through both treadeth down and teareth in pieces, and none can deliver. Thy hand shall be lifted up upon thine adversaries, and all thine enemies shall be cut off. And I will gather my people together as a man gathereth his sheaves into the floor. For I will make my people with whom the Father hath covenanted, yea, I will make thy horn iron, and I will make thy hoofs brass. And thou shalt beat in pieces many people; and I will I consecrate their gain unto the Lord, and their substance unto the Lord of the whole earth. And behold, I am he who doeth it. And it shall come to pass, saith the Father, that the sword of my justice shall hang over them at that day; and except they repent it shall fall upon them, saith the Father, yea, even upon all the nations of the Gentiles. And it shall come to pass that I will establish my people, O house of Israel. And behold, this people I will establish this land, unto the fulfilling of the covenant which I made with your father Jacob; and it shall be a New Jerusalem. And the powers of heaven shall be in the midst of this people; yea, even I will be, in the midst of you. Behold, I am he of whom Moses spake, saying: A prophet shall the Lord your God raise up unto you of your brethren, like unto me; him shall ye hear in all things whatsoever he shall say unto you. And it shall come to pass that every soul who will not hear that prophet shall be cut off from among the people. Verily I say unto you, yea, and all the prophets from Samuel and those that follow after, as many as have spoken, have testified of me. And behold, ye are the children of the prophets; and ye are of the house of Israel; and ye are of the covenant which the Father made with your fathers, saying unto Abraham: And in thy seed shall all the kindreds of the earth be blessed. The Father having raised me up unto you first, and sent me to bless you in turning away every one of you from his iniquities; and this because ye are the children of the covenant—and after that ye were blessed then fulfilleth the Father the covenant which he made with Abraham, saying: In thy seed shall all the kindreds of the earth be blessed—unto the pouring out of the Holy Ghost through me upon the Gentiles, which blessing upon the gentiles shall make them mighty above all, unto the scattering of my people, O house of Israel. And they shall be a scourge unto the people of this land. Nevertheless, when they shall have received the fulness of my gospel, then if they shall harden their hearts against me I will return their iniquities upon their own heads, saith the Father. And I will remember the covenant which I have made with my people; and I have covenanted with them that I would gather them together in mine own due time, that I would give unto them again the land of their fathers for their inheritance, which is the land of Jerusalem, which is the promised land unto them, forever, saith the Father.

And it shall come to pass that the time cometh, when the fulness of my gospel shall be preached unto them; and they shall believe in me, that I am Jesus Christ, the Son of God, and shall pray unto the Father in my name. Then shall their watchmen lift up their voice, and with the voice together shall they sing; for they shall see eye to eye. Then will the Father gather them together again, and give unto them Jerusalem for the land of their inheritance. Then shall they break forth into joy—sing together, ye waste places of Jerusalem; for the Father hath comforted his people, he hath redeemed Jerusalem. The Father hath made bare his holy arm in the eyes of all the nations; and all the ends of the earth shall see the salvation of the Father; and the Father and I are one. And then shall be brought to pass that which is written: Awake, awake again, and put on thy strength, O Zion; put on thy beautiful garments, O

Jerusalem, the holy city, for henceforth there shall no more come into thee the uncircumcised and the unclean. Shake thyself from the dust; arise, sit down, O Jerusalem; loose thyself from the bands of thy neck, O captive daughter of Zion. For thus saith the Lord: Ye have sold yourselves for naught, and ye shall be redeemed without money. Verily, verily, I say unto you, that my people shall know my name; yea, in that day they shall know that I am he that doth speak. And then shall they say: How beautiful upon the mountains are the feet of him that bringeth good tidings unto them, that publisheth peace; that bringeth good tidings unto them of good, that publisheth salvation; that saith unto Zion: Thy God reigneth! And then shall a cry go forth: Depart ye, depart ye, go ye out from thence, touch not that which is unclean; go ye out of the midst of her; be ye clean that bear the vessels of the Lord. For ye shall not go out with haste nor go by flight; for the Lord will go before you, and the God of Israel shall be your rearward. Behold, my servant shall deal prudently; he shall be exalted and extolled and be very high. As many were astonished at thee—his visage was so marred, more than any man, and his form more than the sons of men So shall he sprinkle many nations; the kings shall shut their mouths at him, for that which had not been told them shall they see; and that which they had not heard shall they consider. Verily, verily, I say unto you, all these things shall surely come, even as the Father hath commanded me. Then shall this covenant which the Father hath covenanted with his people be fulfilled; and then shall Jerusalem be inhabited again with my people, and it shall be the land of their inheritance. And verily I say unto you, I give unto you a sign, that he may know when these things shall be about to take place—that I shall gather in, from their long dispersion, my people, O house of Israel, and shall establish again among them my Zion; and behold, this is the thing which I will give unto you for a sign—for verily I say unto you that when these things which I declare unto you, and which I shall declare unto you hereafter of myself, and by the power of the Holy Ghost which shall be given unto you of the Father, shall be made known unto the Gentiles that they may know concerning this people who are a remnant of the house of Jacob, and concerning my people who shall be scattered by them; verily, verily, I say unto you, when these things shall be made unto them of the Father, and shall come forth of the Father, from them unto you; for it is wisdom in the Father that they should be established in this land, and be set up as a free people by the power of the Father, that these things might come forth from them unto a remnant of your seed, that the covenant of the Father may be fulfilled which he hath covenanted with his people, O house of Israel; therefore, when these works and the works which shall be wrought among you hereafter shall come forth from the Gentiles, unto your seed which shall dwindle in unbelief because of iniquity; for thus it behooveth the Father that it should come forth from the Gentiles, that he may show forth his power unto the Gentiles, for this cause that the Gentiles, if they will not harden their hearts, that they may repent and come unto me and be baptized in my name and know of the true points of my doctrine, that they may be numbered among my people, O house of Israel; And when these things come to pass that thy seed shall begin to know these things—it shall be a sign unto them, that they may know that the work of the Father hath already commenced unto the fulfilling of the covenant which he hath made unto the people who are of the house of Israel. And when that day shall come, it shall come to pass that kings shall shut their mouths; for that which had not been told them shall they see; and that which they had not heard shall they consider. For in that day, for my sake shall the Father work a work, which shall be a great and a marvelous work among them; and there shall be among them those who will not believe it, although a man shall declare it unto them. But behold, the life of my servant shall be in my hand; therefore they shall not hurt him, although he shall be marred because of them. Yet I will heal him, for I will show unto them that my wisdom is greater than the cunning of the devil.

Therefore it shall come to pass that whosoever will not believe in my words, who am Jesus Christ, which the Father shall cause him to bring them forth unto the Gentiles, and shall give unto him power that he shall bring them forth unto the Gentiles, (it shall be done even as Moses said) they shall be cut off from among my people who are of the covenant. And my people who are a remnant of Jacob shall be among the Gentiles, yea, in the midst of them as a lion among the beasts of the forest, as a young lion among the flocks of sheep, who, if he go through both treadeth down and teareth in pieces, and none can deliver. Their hand shall be lifted up upon their adversaries, and all their enemies shall be cut off. Yea, wo be unto the Gentiles except they repent; for it shall come to pass in that day, saith the Father, that I will cut off thy horses out of the midst of thee, and I will destroy thy chariots; and I will cut off the cities of thy land, and throw down all thy strongholds; and I will cut off witchcrafts out of thy land, and thou shalt have no more soothsayers; thy graven images I will also cut off, and thy standing images out of the midst of thee, and thou shalt no more worship the works of thy hands; and I will pluck up thy groves out of the midst of thee; so will I destroy thy cities. And it shall come to pass that all lyings, and deceivings, and envyings, and strifes, and priestcrafts, and whoredoms, shall be done away. For it shall come to pass, saith the Father, that at that day whosoever will not repent and come unto my Beloved Son, them will I cut off from among my people, O house of Israel; and I will execute vengeance and fury upon them, even as upon the heathen, such as they have not heard.

CHAPTER X

But if they will repent and hearken unto my words, and harden not their hearts, I will establish my church among them, and they shall come in unto the covenant and be numbered among this the remnant of Jacob, unto whom I have given this land for their inheritance; and they shall assist my people, the remnant of Jacob, and also as many of the house of

Israel as shall come, that they may build a city, which shall be called the New Jerusalem. And then shall they assist my people that they may be gathered in, who are scattered upon all the face of the land, in unto the New Jerusalem. And then shall the power of heaven come down among them; and I also will be in the midst. And then shall the work of the Father commence at that day, even when this gospel shall be preached among the remnant of this people. Verily I say unto you, at that day shall the work of the Father commence among all the dispersed of my people, yea, even the tribes which have been lost, which the Father hath led away out of Jerusalem. Yea, the work shall commence among all the dispersed of my people, with the Father, to prepare the way whereby they may come unto me, that they may call on the Father in my name. Yea, and then shall the work commence, with the Father, among all nations, in preparing the way whereby his people may be gathered home to the land of their inheritance. And they shall go out from all nations; and they shall not go out in haste, nor go by flight, for I will go before them, saith the Father, and I will be their rearward. And then shall that which is written come to pass: Sing, O barren, thou that didst not bear; break forth into singing, and cry aloud, thou that didst not travail with child; for more are the children of the desolate than the children of the married wife, saith the Lord. Enlarge the place of thy tent, and let them stretch forth the curtains of thy habitations; spare not, lengthen thy cords and strengthen thy stakes; for thou shalt break forth on the right hand and on the left, and thy seed shall inherit the Gentiles and make the desolate cities to be inhabited. Fear not, for thou shalt not be ashamed; neither be thou confounded, for thou shalt not be put to shame; for thou shalt forget the shame of thy youth, and shalt not remember the reproach of thy youth, and shalt not remember the reproach of thy widowhood any more. For thy maker, thy husband, the Lord of Hosts is his name; and thy Redeemer, the Holy One of Israel—the God of the whole earth shall he be called. For the Lord hath called thee as a woman forsaken and grieved in spirit, and a wife of youth, when thou wast refused, saith thy God. For a small moment have I forsaken thee, but with great mercies will I gather thee. In a little wrath I hid my face for a moment, but with everlasting kindness will I have mercy on thee, saith the Lord thy Redeemer. For this, the waters of Noah unto me, for as I have sworn that the waters of Noah should no more go over the earth, so have I sworn that I would not be wroth with thee. For the mountains shall depart and the hills be removed, but my kindness shall not depart from thee, neither shall the covenant of my people be removed, saith the Lord that hath mercy on thee.

O thou afflicted, tossed with tempest, and not comforted! Behold, I will lay thy stones with fair colors, and lay thy foundations with sapphires. And I will make thy windows of agates, and thy gates of carbuncles, and all thy borders of pleasant stones. And all thy children shall be taught of the Lord; and great shall be the peace of thy children. In righteousness shalt thou be established; thou shalt be far from oppression for thou shalt not fear, and from terror for it I shall not come near thee. Behold, they shall surely gather together against thee, not by me; whosoever shall gather together against thee shall fall for thy sake. Behold, I have created the smith that bloweth the coals in the fire, and that bringeth forth an instrument for his work; and I have created the waster to destroy. No weapon that is formed against thee shall prosper; and every tongue that shall rise against thee in judgment thou shalt condemn. This is the heritage of the servants of the Lord, and their righteousness is of me, saith the Lord. And now, behold, I say unto you, that ye ought to search these things. Yea, a commandment I give unto you that ye search these things diligently; for great are the words of Isaiah. For surely he spake as touching all things concerning my people which are of the house of Israel; therefore it must needs be that he must speak also to the Gentiles. And all things that he spake have been and shall be, even according to the words which he spake. Therefore give heed to my words; write the things which I have told you; and according to the time and the will of the Father they shall go forth unto the Gentiles. And whosoever will hearken unto my words and repenteth and is baptized, the same shall be saved. Search the prophets, for many there be that testify of these things.

And now it came to pass that when Jesus had said these words he said unto them again, after he had expounded all the scriptures unto them which they had received, he said unto them: Behold, other scriptures I would that ye should write, that ye have not. And it came to pass that he said unto Nephi: Bring forth the record which ye have kept. And when Nephi had brought forth the records, and laid them before him, he cast his eyes upon them and said: Verily I say unto you, I commanded my servant Samuel, the Lamanite, that he should testify unto this people, that at the day that the Father should glorify his name in me that there were many saints who should arise from the dead, and should appear unto many, and should minister unto them. And he said unto them: Was it not so? And his disciples answered him and said: Yea, Lord, Samuel did prophesy according to thy words, and they were all fulfilled. And Jesus said unto them: How be it that ye have not written this thing, that many saints did arise and appear unto many and did minister unto them? And it came to pass that Nephi remembered that this thing had not been written. And it came to pass that Jesus commanded that it should be written; therefore it was written according as he commanded.

CHAPTER XI

And now it came to pass that when Jesus had expounded all the scriptures in one, which they had written, he commanded them that they should teach the things which he had expounded unto them. And it came to pass that he commanded them that they should write the words which the Father had given unto Malachi, which he should tell unto them. And it came to pass that after they were written he expounded them. And these are the words which he did tell unto them, saying:

Thus said the Father unto Malachi—Behold, I will send my
messenger, and he shall prepare the way before me, and the
Lord whom ye seek shall suddenly come to his temple, even
the messenger of the covenant, whom ye delight in; behold, he
shall come, saith the Lord of Hosts. But who may abide the day
of his coming, and who shall stand when he appeareth? For he
is like a refiner's fire, and like fuller's soap. And he shall sit as
a refiner and purifier of silver; and he shall purify the sons of
Levi, and purge them as gold and silver, that they may offer
unto the Lord an offering in righteousness. Then shall the
offering of Judah and Jerusalem be pleasant unto the Lord, as
in the days of old, and as in former years. And I will come near
to you to judgment; and I will be a swift witness against the
sorcerers, and against the adulterers, and against false swear-
ers, and against those that oppress the hireling his wages, the
widow and the fatherless, and that turn aside the stranger, and
fear not me, saith the Lord of Hosts. For I am the Lord, I
change not; therefore ye sons of Jacob are not consumed.

Even from the days of your fathers ye are gone away from
mine ordinances, and have not kept them. Return unto me and
I will return unto you, saith the Lord of Hosts. But ye say:
Wherein shall we return?

Will a man rob God? Yet ye have robbed me. But ye say:
Wherein have we robbed thee? In tithes and offerings. Ye are
cursed with a curse, for ye have robbed me, even this whole
nation. Bring ye all the tithes into the storehouse, that there
may be meat in my house; and prove me now herewith, saith
the Lord of Hosts, if I will not open you the windows of heav-
en, and pour you out a blessing that there shall not be room
enough to receive it. And I will rebuke the devourer for your
sakes, and he shall not destroy the fruits of your ground; neither shall your vine cast her fruit before the time in the fields,
saith the Lord of Hosts. And all nations shall call you blessed,
for ye shall be a delightsome land, saith the Lord of Hosts.

Your words have been stout against me, saith the Lord. Yet
ye say: What have we spoken against thee? Ye have said: It is

vain to serve God, and what doth it profit that we have kept his ordinances and that we have walked mournfully before the Lord of Hosts? And now we call the proud happy; yea, they that work wickedness are set up; yea, they that tempt God are even delivered.

Then they that feared the Lord spake often one to another, and the Lord hearkened and heard; and a book of remembrance was written before him for them that feared the Lord, and that thought upon his name. And they shall be mine, saith the Lord of Hosts, in that day when I make up my jewels; and I will spare them as a man spareth his own son that serveth him. Then shall ye return and discern between the righteous and the wicked, between him that serveth God and him that serveth him not. For behold, the day cometh that shall burn as an oven; and all the proud, yea, and all that do wickedly, shall be stubble; and the day that cometh shall burn them up, saith the Lord of Hosts, that it shall leave them neither root nor branch.

But unto you that fear my name, shall the Son of Righteousness arise with healings in his wings; and ye shall go forth and grow up as calves in the stall. And ye shall tread down the wicked; for they shall be ashes under the soles of your feet in the day that I shall do this, saith the Lord of Hosts. Remember ye the law of Moses, my servant, which I commanded unto him in Horeb for all Israel, with the statutes and judgments. Behold, I will send you Elijah the prophet before the coming of the great and dreadful day of the Lord; and he shall turn the heart of the fathers to the children, and the heart of the children to their fathers, lest I come and smite the earth with a curse.

And now it came to pass that when Jesus had told these things he expounded them unto the multitude; and he did expound all things unto them, both great and small. And he saith: These scriptures, which ye had not with you, the Father commanded that I should give unto to you; for it was wisdom in him that they should be given unto future generations. And he did expound all things, even from the beginning until the time that he should come in his glory—yea, even all things which should come upon the face of the earth, even until the elements should melt with fervent heat, and the earth should be wrapt together as a scroll, and the heavens and the earth should pass away; and even unto the great and last day, when all people, and all kindreds, and all nations and tongues shall stand before God to be judged of their works, whether they be good or whether they be evil—if they be good, to the resurrection of everlasting life; and if they be evil, to the resurrection of damnation; being on a parallel, the one on the one hand and the other on the other hand, according to the mercy, and the justice, and the holiness which is in Christ, who was before the world began.

CHAPTER XII

And now there cannot be written in this book even a hundredth part of the things which Jesus did truly teach unto the people; but behold the plates of Nephi do contain the more part of the things which he taught the people. And these things have I written, which are a lesser part of the things which he taught the people; and I have written them to the intent that they may be brought again unto this people, from the Gentiles, according to the words which Jesus hath spoken. And when they shall have received this, which is expedient that they should have first, to try their faith, and if it shall so be that they shall believe these things then shall the greater things be made manifest unto them. And if it so be that they will not believe these things, then shall the greater things be withheld from them, unto their condemnation. Behold, I was about to write them, all which were engraven upon the plates of Nephi, but the Lord forbade it, saying: I will try the faith of my people. Therefore I, Mormon, do write the things which have been commanded me of the Lord. And now I, Mormon, make an end of my sayings, and proceed to write the things which have been commanded me. Therefore, I would that ye should behold that the Lord truly did teach the people, for the space of three days; and after that he did show himself unto them oft, and did break bread oft, and bless it, and give it unto them.

And it came to pass that he did teach and minister unto the children of the multitude of whom hath been spoken, and he did loose their tongues, and they did speak unto their fathers great and marvelous things, even greater than he had revealed unto the people; and he loosed their tongues that they could utter. And it came to pass that after he had ascended into heaven the second time that he showed himself unto them, and had gone unto the Father, after having healed all their sick, and their lame, and opened the eyes of their blind and unstopped the ears of the deaf, and even had done all manner of cures among them, and raised a man from the dead, and had shown forth his power unto them, and had ascended unto the Father-Behold, it came to pass on the morrow that the multitude gathered themselves together, and they both saw and heard these children; yea, even babes did open their mouths and utter marvelous things; and the things which they did utter were forbidden that there should not any man write them.

And it came to pass that the disciples whom Jesus had chosen began from that time forth to baptize and to teach as many as did come unto them; and as many as were baptized in the name of Jesus were filled with the Holy Ghost. And many of them saw and heard unspeakable things, which are not lawful to be written. And they taught, and did minister one to another; and they had all things common among them, every man dealing justly, one with another. And it came to pass that they did do all things even as Jesus had commanded them. And they who were baptized in the name of Jesus were called the church of Christ.

And it came to pass that as the disciples of Jesus were journeying and were preaching the things which they had both heard and seen, and were baptizing in the name of Jesus, it came to pass that the disciples were gathered together and were united in mighty prayer and fasting. And Jesus again showed himself unto them, for they were praying unto the Father in his name; and Jesus came and stood in the midst of them, and said unto them: What will ye that I shall give unto you? And they said unto him: Lord, we will that thou wouldst tell us the name whereby we shall call this church; for there are disputations among the people concerning this matter. And the Lord said unto them: Verily, verily, I say unto you, why is it that the people should murmur and dispute because of this thing? Have they not read the scriptures, which say ye must take upon you the name of Christ, which is my name? For by this name shall ye be called at the last day; and whoso taketh upon him my name, and endureth to the end, the same shall be saved at the last day. Therefore, whatsoever ye shall do, ye shall do it in my name; therefore ye shall call the church in my name; and ye shall call upon the Father in my name that he will bless the church for my sake. And how be it my church save it be called in my name? For if a church be called in Moses' name then it be Moses' church; or if it be called in the name of a man then it be the church of a man; but if it be called in my name then it is my church, if it so be that they are built upon my gospel. Verily I say unto you, that ye are built upon my gospel; therefore ye shall call whatsoever things ye do call, in my name; therefore if ye call upon the Father, for the church, if it be in my name the Father will hear you; and if it so be that the church is built upon my gospel, then will the Father show forth his own works in it. But if it be not built upon my gospel, and is built upon the works of men, or upon the works of the devil, verily I say unto you they have joy in their works for a season, and by and by the end cometh, and they are hewn down and cast into the fire, from whence there is no return. For their works do follow them for it is because of their works that they are hewn down; therefore remember the things that I have told you. Behold I have given unto you my gospel, and this is the gospel which I have given unto you—that I came into the world to do the will of my Father, because my Father sent me. And my Father sent me that I might be lifted up upon the cross; and after that I had been lifted up upon the cross, that I might draw all men unto me, that as I have been lifted up by men even so should men be lifted up by the Father, to stand before me, to be judged of their works, whether they be good or whether they be evil—and for this cause have I been lifted up; therefore, according to the power of the Father I will draw all men unto me, that they may be judged according to their works. And it shall come to pass, that whoso repenteth and is baptized in my name shall be filled; and if he endureth to the end, behold, him will I hold guiltless before my Father at that day when I shall stand to judge the world. And he that endureth not unto the end, the same is he that is also hewn down and cast into the fire, from whence they can no more return, because of the justice of the Father. And this is the word which he hath given unto the children of men. And for this cause he fulfilleth the words which he hath given, and he lieth not, but fulfilleth all his words. And no unclean thing can enter into his kingdom; therefore nothing entereth into his rest save it be those who have washed their garments in my blood, because of their faith, and the repentance of all their sins and their faithfulness unto the end. Now this is the commandment: Repent, all ye ends of the earth, and come unto me and be baptized in my name, that ye may be sanctified by the reception of the Holy Ghost, that ye may stand spotless before me at the last day. Verily, verily, I say unto you, this is my gospel; and ye know the things that ye must do in my church; for the works which ye have seen me do that shall ye also do; for that which ye have seen me do even that shall ye do; therefore, if ye do these things blessed are ye, for ye shall be lifted up at the last day.

CHAPTER XIII

Write the things which ye have seen and heard, save it be those which are forbidden. Write the works of this people, which shall be, even as hath been written, of that which hath been. For behold, out of the books which have been written, and which shall be written, shall this people be judged, for by them shall their works be known unto men. And behold, all things are written by the Father; therefore out of the books which shall be written shall the world judged. And know ye that ye shall be judges of this people, according to the judgment which I shall give unto you, which shall be just. Therefore, what manner of men ought ye to be? Verily I say unto you, even as I even as I am. And now I go unto the Father. I say unto you, whatsoever things ye shall ask the Father in my name shall be given unto you. Therefore, ask, and ye shall receive; knock, and it shall be opened unto you; for he that asketh, receiveth; and unto him that knocketh, it shall be opened. And now, behold, my joy is great, even unto fulness, because of you, and also this generation; yea, and even the Father rejoiceth, and also all the holy angels, because of you and this generation; for none of them are lost. Behold, I would that ye should understand; for I mean them who are now alive of this generation; and none of them are lost; and in them I have fulness of joy. But behold, it sorroweth me because of the fourth generation from this generation, for they are led away captive by him even as was the son of perdition; for they will sell me for silver and for gold, and for that which moth doth corrupt and which thieves can break through and steal. And in that day will I visit them, even in turning their works upon their own heads.

And it came to pass that when Jesus had ended these sayings he said unto his disciples: Enter ye in at the strait gate; for strait is the gate, and narrow is the way that leads to life, and few there be that find it; but wide is the gate, and broad the way which leads to death, and many there be that travel therein, until the night cometh, wherein no man can work.

And it came to pass when Jesus had said these words, he spake unto his disciples, one by one, saying unto them: What is it that ye desire of me, after that I am gone to the Father? And they all spake, save it were three, saying: We desire that after we have lived unto the age of man, that our ministry, wherein thou hast called us, may have an end, that we may speedily come unto thee in thy kingdom. And he said unto them: Blessed are ye because ye desired this thing of me; therefore, after that ye are seventy and two years old ye shall come unto me in my kingdom; and with me ye shall find rest. And when he had spoken unto them, he turned himself unto the three, and said unto them: What will ye that I should do unto you, when I am gone unto the Father? And they sorrowed in their hearts, for they durst not speak unto him the thing which they desired. And he said unto them: Behold, I know your thoughts, and ye have desired the thing which John, my beloved, who was with me in my ministry, before that I was lifted up by the Jews, desired of me. Therefore, more blessed are ye, for ye shall never taste of death; but ye shall live to behold all the doings of the Father unto the children of men, even until all things shall be fulfilled according to the will of the Father, when I shall come in my glory with the powers of heaven. And ye shall never endure the pains of death; but when I shall come in my glory ye shall be changed in the twinkling of an eye from mortality to immortality; and then shall ye be blessed in the kingdom of my Father. And again, ye shall not have pain while ye shall dwell in the flesh, neither sorrow save it be for the sins of the world; and all this will I do because of the thing which ye have desired of me, for ye have desired that ye might bring the souls of men unto me, while the world shall stand. And for this cause ye shall have fulness of joy; and ye shall sit down in the kingdom of my Father; yea, your joy shall be full, even as the Father hath given me fulness of joy; and ye shall be even as I am, and I am even as the Father; and the Father and I are one; and the Holy Ghost beareth record of the Father and me; and the Father giveth the Holy Ghost unto the children of men, because of me.

And it came to pass that when Jesus had spoken these words, he touched every one of them with his finger save it were the three who were to tarry, and then he departed. And behold, the heavens were opened, and they were caught up into heaven, and saw and heard unspeakable things.

CHAPTER XIV

Hearken, O ye Gentiles, and hear the words of Jesus Christ, the Son of the living God, which he hath commanded me that I should speak concerning you, for, behold he commandeth me that I should write, saying:

Turn, all ye Gentiles, from your wicked ways; and repent of your evil doings, of your lyings and deceivings, and of your whoredoms, and of your secret abominations, and your idolatries, and of your murders, and your priestcrafts, and your envyings, and your strifes, and from all your wickedness and abominations, and come unto me, and be baptized in my name, that ye may receive a remission of your sins, and be filled with the Holy Ghost, that ye may be numbered with my people who are of the house of Israel.

References

Bancroft, Hubert Howe. *The Native Races, Five Volumes.* San Francisco: A. L. Bancroft & Company, Publishers, 1883.

Castillo, Bernal Dias del. *The Discovery and Conquest of Mexico* (New York 1956).

Book of Commandments for the Government of the Church of Christ, Zion. Published by W. W. Phelps & Co. 1833.

Brading, D. A. *The First America.* Cambridge University Press, 1991.

Chronicles, Bernal Diaz, The True Story of the Conquest of Mexico. Translated and edited by Albert Idell. Doubleday & Company, Inc., Garden City, New York, 1957.

Conquistadors, The, First-person accounts of the Conquest of Mexico (Including the writings of Juan Diaz, Andres de Tapia, Hernan Cortes, Pedro de Alvarado). Edited and translated by Patricia de Fuentes, Preface by Howard F. Cline, Director, The Hispanic Foundation, Library of Congress. The Orion Press, New York.

Cortes, Hernan. *Letters From Mexico.* Translated and edited by A.R. Pagden, with an Introduction by J. H. Elliott, an Orion Press Book. Grossman Publishers, New York.

De Roo, P. *History of America Before Columbus.* Philadelphia and London, J. D. Lippincott Company.

Dibble, Charles E. *The Conquest Through Aztec Eyes*. The 41st Annual Frederick William Reynolds Lecture. University of Utah Press, Salt Lake City, Utah, 1978.

Duran, Fray Diego. *Aztecs, The History of the Indies of New Spain*. Translated, with notes, by Doris Heyden and Fernando Horcasitas. Orion Press, New York.

Duran, Fray Diego. *Book of the Gods and Rites and the The Ancient Calendar*. Translated and edited by Fernando Horcasitas and Doris Heyden, Forword by Miguel Leon-Portilla. University of Oklahoma Press.

Gomara, Francisco Lopez de, Cortes. *The Life of the Conqueror by His Secretary*. Translated and Edited by Lesley Byrd Simpson, from the Istoria de La Conquista be Mexico, Printed in Zaragoza, 1552, University of California Press, Berkeley and Los Angeles, 1964.

Gomara, Francisco Lopez. *The Conquest of West India (1578)*. With an Introduction by Herbert Ingram Priestley, Director, Bancroft Library, University of California, Scholars' Facsimiles and Reprints. New York. N. Y., 1940.

Hammond, Norman and Willey, Gordon R. *Maya Archaeology and Ethnohistory*. University of Texas Press, Austin and London.

Ixtlilxochitl, Fernando de Alva. *Ally of Cortes, Account 13: of the coming of the Spaniards and the beginning of the evangelical law*. Translated with a Foreword by Douglass, K. Ballentine. Texas Western Press, The University of Texas at El Paso.

Ixtlilxochitl, Fernando de Alva. *Obras Historicas, Vol. I and Vol. II*. Ed. Edmundo O'Gorman, Translated by Ronda Cunningham. Universidad Nacional Autonoma de Mexico, Mexico, 1975.

Kingsborough, Edward King, Lord. *Antiquities of Mexico*, nine volumes. Published by Robert Havell, 77 Oxford St. London, Printed by James Moyes, Castle St., Leicester Square, and Colnaghi, Son, and Co. Pall Mall East, 1831-1848, London, England.

LaFaye, Jacques. *Quetzalcoatl and Guadalupe*. Foreword by Octavio Paz, Translated by Benjamin Keen. The University of Chicago Press.

Landa, Friar Diego de. *Yucatan Before and After the Conquest*. Translated with notes by William Gates. Dover Publications, Inc. New York.

Landa's Relacion de Las Cosas de Yucatan. Papers of the Peabody Museum of American Archaelogy and Ethology, Harvard University, Vol XVIII, a translation, Edited and Notes by Alfred M. Tozzer, Cambridge, Massachusetts, U.S.A. Published by the Museum, 1941.

Leon-Portilla, Miguel. *PreColumbian Literatures of Mexico*. Translated from the Spanish by Grace Lobanov and the Author. University of Oklahoma Press, Norman.

Mendieta, Fray Geronimo de. *Historia Eclesiastica Indiana, Obra escrita a Fines del Siglo XVI*. Mexico, Antigua Libreria, Portal de Agustinos No. 3.

Motolinia, Fray Toribio de Benavente. *Motolinia's History of the Indians of New Spain*. Translated and edited by Elizabeth Andros Foster, Ph.D. The Cortes Society. 1950.

Prescott, William H., *History of the Conquest of Mexico and History of the Conquest of Peru*, The Modern Library, New York

Sahagun, Fray Bernardino de. *A History of Ancient Mexico*. Translated by Fanny R. Bandelier, from the Spanish version of Carlos Maria de Bustamante. The Rio Grande Press, Inc.

Sahagun, Fray Bernardino de, Florentine Codex. *General History of the Things of New Spain*. Translated from the Aztec into English with notes and illustrations by Arthur J. G. Anderson and Charles E. Dibble. Published by The School of American Research and the University of Utah; Monographs of the School of American Research, Santa Fe, New Mexico.

Taylor, John. *Mediation and Atonement*. Deseret News Company, Salt Lake City, Utah 1882.

Vega, Garcilaso de la, El Inca. *Royal Commentaries of the Incas, and General History of Peru*. Translated with an Introduction by Harold V. Livermore, Part Two. University of Texas Press, Austin and London.

Veytia, Don Mariano Fernandez de Echevarria y. *Ancient America Rediscovered*. First Translation of a portion of his two volume work titled *Historia Antigua de Mexico*. Translation by Ronda Cunningham, Bonneville Books, Cedar Fort Inc. Springville, Utah, 84663, 2000.

Willard, T. A. *Kukulcan, The Bearded Conqueror, New Mayan Discoveries*. With Illustrations from Original Photographs. Murray and Gee, Hollywood.

Index

A

Adultery, thou shalt not commit 58, 74, 144

American Indians of Jewish descent 81, 126, 129

Analogies of belief and ritual between Mexico and Christianity

which resulted from ancient evangelization of America 122

Analogies between Quetzalcoatl in conduct, aspect, and speech to those of an apostle of Christ 70

Ascension of Jesus into heaven 158, 178

Aztecs—Mexicans 5, 8

Preparation of Aztec mind, Strange omens preceding the coming of Cortes 8

What did these omens mean? 11

B

Bancroft, Hubert Howe, reviewed Book of Mormon 95

Baptism, taught by Jesus Christ 140, 141, 148

Baptism in ancient language means being born again 76

Before baptism, children they asked if they had sinned 76

Children often given a name at baptism 75, 83

Aztec baptism 99

In some towns baptism was done not by infusion but by immersion, submerging the children in ponds, rivers, springs or fonts full of water 77

Quetzalcoatl taught them this ablution or bath of natural water 77, 78

Throughout this country a type of baptism was found to be established. 77

Baptism with the Holy Ghost 136

Birth of Jesus Christ, 4034 years of the world 53, 55

Suspension of the sun, night and day of continuous light at birth of Son of God 131

New star appeared 131

C

Christ visited the people of Book of Mormon after his ascension

in Palestine 56, 57, 138, 139

Christ blessed little children 154

Church called in my name (Jesus Christ) 174

Circumcision practiced 81

superceded by baptism 83

Communion, Christian 155, 161

Corn bread made into the form of a human being; priests would bless it, and the people ate pieces of it as though eating the flesh of their God. 79, 80, 155

Cortes, Don Hernando 1, 2

Considered to be a god, Quetzalcoatl, by Montezuma 23, 24, 25

Signs and wonders before coming of Cortes 8-10, 49

Cross, holy, venerated since very early times 63, 65, 66, 67, 89

Cordoba discovered Yucatan 3

D

Death of Jesus Christ, events at, tempests, earthquakes, whirl-wind before appearance of Jesus Christ 52, 53, 130-133

Thick darkness on face of land for three days 52, 132, 133

Only more righteous people were saved 137

Devil, it was all of the 116, 117

Disciples of Jesus Christ given authority to baptize 142

Doctrines of Trinity and Virgin birth 59, 62, 103

Doctrine of Father, Son, and Holy Ghost 62, 141

E

Eclipse and earthquake at time of death of Jesus Christ,

three days total darkness. 52, 53, 130-133

Existence of God 70

F

Fast established by Quetzalcoatl 44, 59, 74

First people in Mexico, seven families, at time of changing of

languages 47

Constructed high tower 86

Flood, world destroyed by, 46

G

Giants 41, 48

Gospel, definition of 175, 176

Grijalva preceded Cortes 3, 15

H

Heal the sick and give sight to the blind 153

Historians declared that a white man preached among them a holy law 42, 44

Huemac—Quetzalcoatl, are same person 42. 44

I

Indian believed there was a universal God of all things, creator of them,

Lord of Heaven and earth, one just God 43, 46, 70, 71, 74

believed Christian doctrine 82

Ixtlilxochitl, Fernando de Alva, historian 39

J

Jesus Christ descended out of heaven 139

clothed in a white robe, ankle length tunic 56, 139

taught whatsoever you would have men do to you, do unto them 148

be even as I am 176

be perfect as I and my Father are 145

healed the sick, lame, blind,

and halt 150, 153

taught to pray always in his name 156

pray after this manner 145

ascended into heaven 158, 178

taught mercy, justice and holiness 59, 92, 101

love your enemies 145

Jesus Christ, the Son of God 135, 163

Slain for sins of the world 140

Judgment, men to be judged according to their works 175

K

Kill, thou shalt not 119, 143

Kingsborough, Lord Edward King, Quetzalcoatl was greatest of their gods 101

L

Law of Moses fulfilled 136, 149

Love your enemies 145

M

Man is in the image of God 110

Mayan words corresponding with Christian faith 116

Messiah, arguments identified Quetzalcoatl with 94

Mexicans paintings show Christ crucified 113, 114

Quetzalcoatl crucified and nailed to the cross 114

Mexicans believed many doctrinesheld to be peculiarly and exclusively Christian 102

Montezuma, Aztec Emperor 11

Montezuma thought Cortes was a god Quetzalcoatl 19

Moses, law of, fulfilled 136, 149

N

Nephites (inhabitants of America as related in the Book of Mormon)

informed of birth and death of Jesus Christ 139, 140

received a visit from Christ after his ascension in Palestine 139

A new star appeared at the birth of Jesus Christ 131

O

Origin of native Americans, theories 95

Other sheep I have which are not of this fold nor in Jerusalem, said Jesus Christ 150

P

Pray in my name, said Jesus Christ 156

Prescott, William Hickling, historian 98

Q

Quetzalcoatl, a white, bearded man of good stature 56, 92, 98, 111

wore white, ankle-length tunic 56

considered a sorcerer by Torquemada 58

Quetzalcohuatl, Colcolcan, [Kukulcan] and Hueman,

the same wonderful man, 44, 51, 146, 147

An ancient revered God throughout middle America 42, 44, 59, 62, 92, 101, 103

Other names for him 93, 120

Topiltzin, another name for Quetzalcohuatl, might be interpreted Son of Man 108

Quetzalcoatl was Jesus Christ 93, 94, 125

all-powerful divinity, symbol of divine wisdom, of most lofty spiritual thought in ancient Mexico, 121, 122

R
Resurrection of the body 103, 107

Repent of your evil ways 178

S
Sacrament of the Lords Supper

Jesus blessed and gave wine in remembrance of blood He had shed for them, broke bread and gave to multitude in remembrance of His body 79, 99, 155, 161

Sahagun, great scholar, declared Quetzalcoatl, God of Toltecs, creator, teacher and Lord 119

Supreme God in Heaven, although He was just one, there were three persons 71, 72, 103, 178

T
Taylor, John president of The Church of Jesus Christ of Latter day Saints 1880-1887 stated "Quetzal-coatl and Christ are same being " 125

Toltecs came to Mexico at the time of confusion of languages 46, 47

Trinity, doctrine of Father, Son , and Holy Ghost 62, 71, 72, 103, 178

U
Uses, customs and traditions established throughout New Spain which by very ancient tradition had to have been introduced by Quetzalcoatl 73

V
Veytia, Don Mariano Fernandez de Echevarria Y, Mexican Historian 52

Votan, closely resembling Quetzalcohuatl was the supposed founder of Maya civilization 93

Z
Zamna and Cuculkan were in Yucatan 93

About the Compiler

Donald W. Hemingway is an attorney, teacher, musician, and author. He received an AB in music from Brigham Young University in 1942 and a JD from the University of Southern California in 1948. He has practiced law in Nevada and Utah and worked many years as Judge Advocate in the United States Air Force, specializing in government contract law, retiring as a Lieutenant Colonel.

Of his World War II experience serving in Egypt, North Africa, and Italy, he wrote: *Private Hemingway Goes to War.* He also published a scriptural story of Jesus of Nazareth *Follow Me,* and a historical novel *Joseph Smith: A Prophet—Prayer with a Promise.* This book is the third in a series concerning Mexican history and the Book of Mormon. The first were *Christianity in America Before Columbus?* and with his son W. David Hemingway, *Ancient America Rediscovered,* a translation of a portion of *Historia Antigua de Mexico* by Mariano Veytia. He has also written many legal papers in his specialized field of law.

For years he has taught church history and scriptures on the high school and college levels.

He and his wife Donna have six children, thirty-four grandchildren, and five great grandchildren, at the moment.